THE YALE SHAKESPEARE

Revised Edition

General Editors

Helge Kökeritz and Charles T. Prouty

THE YALE SHAKESPEARE

THE TRAGEDY OF ANTONY
AND CLEOPATRA

Edited by Peter G. Phialas

NEW HAVEN AND LONDON
YALE UNIVERSITY PRESS

Preface of the General Editors

AS the late Professor Tucker Brooke has observed, practically all modern editions of Shakespeare are 18th-century versions of the plays, based on the additions, alterations, and emendations of editors of that period. It has been our purpose, as it was Professor Brooke's, to give the modern reader Shakespeare's plays in the approximate form of their original appearance.

About half the plays appeared in quarto form before the publication of the First Folio in 1623. Thus for a large number of plays the only available text is that of the Folio. In the case of quarto plays our policy has been to use that text as the basis of the edition, unless it is clear that the text has been contaminated.

Interesting for us today is the fact that there are no act or scene divisions in the Quartos with the exception of *Othello*, which does mark Acts I, II, IV, and V but lacks indications of scenes. Even in the Folio, although act divisions are generally noted, only a part of the scenes are divided. In no case, either in Quarto or Folio, is there any indication of the place of action. The manifold scene divisions for the battle in such a play as *Antony and Cleopatra*, together with such locations as "Another part of the field," are the additions of the 18th century.

We have eliminated all indications of the place and time of action, because there is no authority for them in the originals and because Shakespeare gives such information, when it is requisite for understanding the play, through the dialogue of the actors. We have been sparing in our use of added scene and, in some cases, act divisions, because these frequently impede the flow of the action, which in Shakespeare's time was curiously like that of modern films.

Spelling has been modernized except when the original clearly indicates a pronunciation unlike our own, e.g. *desart* (desert), *divel* (devil), *banket* (banquet), and often in such Elizabethan syncopations as *ere* (e'er), *stolne* (stol'n), and *tane* (ta'en). In reproducing such forms we have followed the inconsistent usage of the original.

We have also preserved the original capitalization when this is a part of the meaning. In like manner we have tended to adopt the lineation of the original in many cases where modern editors print prose as verse or verse as prose. We have, moreover, followed the original punctuation wherever it was practicable.

In verse we print a final *-ed* to indicate its full syllabic value, otherwise *'d*. In prose we have followed the inconsistencies of the original in this respect.

Our general practice has been to include in footnotes all information a reader needs for immediate understanding of the given page. In somewhat empiric fashion we repeat glosses as we think the reader needs to be reminded of the meaning. Further information is given in notes (indicated by the letter *N* in the footnotes) to be found at the back of each volume. Appendices deal with the text and sources of the play.

Square brackets indicate material not found in the original text. Long emendations or lines taken from another authoritative text of a play are indicated in the footnotes for the information of the reader. We have silently corrected obvious typographical errors.

At the risk of inconsistency, we have followed the Folio text of *Antony and Cleopatra* and have omitted all act and scene divisions usually found in modern editions. These derive from various 18th-century editors and have the effect of impeding the rapid flow of action which is so much a part of the structure of this play. The traditional line numbering has been preserved, and the traditional act and scene divisions are noted in the top margin and in the glosses, so that easy reference to quoted matter and the like is available.

CONTENTS

[THE ACTORS' NAMES

MARK ANTONY
OCTAVIUS CAESAR } *triumvirs*
M. AEMILIUS LEPIDUS

DOMITIUS ENOBARBUS
VENTIDIUS
EROS
SCARUS } *friends to Antony*
DERCETAS
DEMETRIUS
PHILO

MAECENAS
AGRIPPA
DOLABELLA
PROCULEIUS } *friends to Caesar*
THIDIAS
GALLUS

MENAS
MENECRATES } *friends to Pompey*
VARRIUS

TAURUS, *lieutenant general to Caesar*
CANIDIUS, *lieutenant general to Antony*
ROMAN OFFICER UNDER VENTIDIUS
A SCHOOLMASTER

ALEXAS
MARDIAN
SELEUCUS } *attendants on Cleopatra*
DIOMEDES

A SOOTHSAYER
A CLOWN
CLEOPATRA, *Queen of Egypt*
OCTAVIA, *sister to Caesar, and wife to Antony*

CHARMIAN } *attendants on Cleopatra*
IRAS

Officers, Soldiers, Messengers, Attendants]

THE TRAGEDY OF ANTONY
AND CLEOPATRA

Enter Demetrius and Philo.

Philo. Nay, but this dotage of our general's
O'erflows the measure: those his goodly eyes,
That o'er the files and musters of the war
Have glow'd like plated Mars, now bend, now turn
The office and devotion of their view   5
Upon a tawny front. His captain's heart,
Which in the scuffles of great fights hath burst
The buckles on his breast, reneges all temper,   8
And is become the bellows and the fan
To cool a gypsy's lust.

*Flourish. Enter Antony, Cleopatra, her Ladies,
the train, with Eunuchs fanning her.*

                    Look! where they come:
Take but good note, and you shall see in him
The triple pillar of the world transform'd   12
Into a strumpet's fool. Behold and see.
Cleopatra. If it be love indeed, tell me how much.

---

4 plated clothed in armor. **5 office** service. **6 tawny front** dark face.
8 reneges renounces. **temper** self-restraint. **10 gypsy's** N. (N
refers throughout to the corresponding note given at the end of
the text.) **12 triple pillar** N. **13 fool** dupe.

Antony. There's beggary in the love that can be
    reckon'd.   15
Cleopatra. I'll set a bourn how far to be belov'd.
Antony. Then must thou needs find out new heaven,
    new earth.

Enter a Messenger.

Messenger. News, my good lord, from Rome.
Antony.   Grates me, the sum.
Cleopatra. Nay, hear them, Antony.
Fulvia, perchance, is angry: or, who knows   20
If the scarce-bearded Caesar have not sent
His powerful mandate to you, 'Do this, or this;
Take in that kingdom, and enfranchise that.
Perform't, or else we damn thee.'
Antony.   How, my love?   24
Cleopatra. Perchance? nay, and most like:
You must not stay here longer, your dismission
Is come from Caesar; therefore hear it, Antony. 27
Where's Fulvia's process? Caesar's I would say?
    both?
Call in the messengers. As I am Egypt's queen,
Thou blushest, Antony, and that blood of thine 30
Is Caesar's homager: else so thy cheek pays shame
When shrill-tongu'd Fulvia scolds. The messengers!
Antony. Let Rome in Tiber melt, and the wide arch
Of the rang'd empire fall! Here is my space.
Kingdoms are clay: our dungy earth alike
Feeds beast as man; the nobleness of life   36

15 **beggary** N. 16 **bourn** boundary. 18 **Grates** irritates. **the sum**
be brief. 20 **Fulvia** Antony's wife. 21 **scarce-bearded** N. 23 **Take
in** conquer. **enfranchise** set free. 25 **most like** without doubt.
26 **dismission** dismissal. 28 **process** summons. 31 **homager** vassal.
34 **rang'd** 'well-ordered'; or possibly, 'far-flung.'

2

Is to do thus: when such a mutual pair
And such a twain can do't, in which I bind,
On pain of punishment, the world to weet
We stand up peerless.

Cleopatra.   Excellent falsehood!   40
Why did he marry Fulvia and not love her?
I'll seem the fool I am not. Antony will be himself.

Antony. But stirr'd by Cleopatra.
Now, for the love of Love and her soft hours,   44
Let's not confound the time with conference harsh;
There's not a minute of our lives should stretch
Without some pleasure now. What sport tonight?

Cleopatra. Hear the ambassadors.

Antony.   Fie, wrangling queen!
Whom everything becomes, to chide, to laugh,   49
To weep: whose every passion fully strives
To make itself (in thee) fair and admir'd.
No messenger but thine, and all alone tonight   52
We'll wander through the streets, and note
The qualities of people. Come, my queen.
Last night you did desire it. Speak not to us.   55
                    Exeunt with the train.

Demetrius. Is Caesar with Antonius priz'd so slight?

Philo. Sir, sometimes when he is not Antony
He comes too short of that great property
Which still should go with Antony.

Demetrius.   I am full sorry

37 **mutual** with equal love for each other. 39 **to weet** to know,
to acknowledge. 42 **I'll seem . . . not** I'll pretend I am foolish
enough to believe you (which I am not really). 45 **confound** waste.
46 **stretch** pass, be protracted. 50 **whose** F *who.* (F refers throughout to the First Folio of 1623.) **passion** emotion. 52–4 **all alone
. . . people** N. 54 **qualities** characteristics. 58 **property** distinctive
quality.

That he approves the common liar, who   60
Thus speaks of him at Rome; but I will hope
Of better deeds tomorrow. Rest you happy!
                                    Exeunt.

*Enter Enobarbus, a Soothsayer, Charmian, Iras,
        Mardian the eunuch, and Alexas.*

Charmian. Lord Alexas, sweet Alexas, most any-
thing Alexas, almost most absolute Alexas, where's
the soothsayer that you prais'd so to th' queen? O,
that I knew this husband, which, you say, must
change his horns with garlands.   5
Alexas. Soothsayer!
Soothsayer. Your will?
Charmian. Is this the man? Is't you, sir, that know
things?   9
Soothsayer. In nature's infinite book of secrecy a
little I can read.
Alexas. Show him your hand.   12
Enobarbus. Bring in the banket quickly: wine
enough Cleopatra's health to drink.
Charmian. Good sir, give me good fortune.
Soothsayer. I make not, but foresee.   16
Charmian. Pray then, foresee me one.
Soothsayer. You shall be yet far fairer than you
are.
Charmian. He means in flesh.   20
Iras. No, you shall paint when you are old.
Charmian. Wrinkles forbid!
Alexas. Vex not his prescience, be attentive.

60 **approves** proves true. 62 **Rest you happy** May God keep you
happy. SD **Enter Enobarbus** begins I.2 N. (SD is used throughout to indicate stage direction.) 2 **absolute** perfect. 5 **change . . .
garlands** N. 13 **banket** banquet, dessert.
          4

Charmian. Hush!   24

Soothsayer. You shall be more beloving than belov'd.

Charmian. I had rather heat my liver with drinking.

Alexas. Nay, hear him.   27

Charmian. Good now, some excellent fortune: let me be married to three kings in a forenoon, and widow them all: let me have a child at fifty, to whom Herod of Jewry may do homage. Find me to marry me with Octavius Caesar, and companion me with my mistress.

Soothsayer. You shall outlive the lady whom you serve.   34

Charmian. O excellent! I love long life better than figs.   36

Soothsayer. You have seen and prov'd a fairer former fortune

Than that which is to approach.

Charmian. Then belike my children shall have no names. Prithee, how many boys and wenches must I have?   41

Soothsayer. If every of your wishes had a womb, And fertile every wish, a million.

Charmian. Out, fool! I forgive thee for a witch.   44

Alexas. You think none but your sheets are privy to your wishes.

Charmian. Nay, come, tell Iras hers.

Alexas. We'll know all our fortunes.   48

Enobarbus. Mine, and most of our fortunes, to-night, shall be—drunk to bed.

---

26 heat . . . drinking N. 30–1 Herod of Jewry N. 32 companion me i.e. as the wife of a triumvir. 35–6 I . . . figs N. 37 prov'd experienced. 39–40 shall have no names will be bastards. 40 wenches girls. 43 fertile F *foretell.* 44 for because you are. 45–6 privy to secretly aware of.

Iras. There's a palm presages chastity, if nothing else.   52

Charmian. E'en as the o'erflowing Nilus presageth famine.

Iras. Go, you wild bedfellow, you cannot soothsay.

Charmian. Nay, if an oily palm be not a fruitful prognostication, I cannot scratch mine ear. Prithee, tell her but a worky-day fortune.   58

Soothsayer. Your fortunes are alike.

Iras. But how, but how? give me particulars.

Soothsayer. I have said.   61

Iras. Am I not an inch of fortune better than she?

Charmian. Well, if you were but an inch of fortune better than I, where would you choose it?

Iras. Not in my husband's nose.   65

Charmian. Our worser thoughts Heavens mend! Alexas, come, his fortune, his fortune. O, let him marry a woman that cannot go, sweet Isis, I beseech thee, and let her die too, and give him a worse, and let worse follow worse, till the worst of all follow him laughing to his grave, fifty-fold a cuckold. Good Isis, hear me this prayer, though thou deny me a matter of more weight: good Isis, I beseech thee.   73

Iras. Amen, dear goddess, hear that prayer of the people. For, as it is a heart-breaking to see a handsome man loose-wiv'd, so it is a deadly sorrow to behold a foul knave uncuckolded. Therefore, dear Isis, keep decorum, and fortune him accordingly.

Charmian. Amen.   79

51 **presages chastity** because it is dry and cool. 56 **oily palm** believed to indicate wantonness. 56–7 **fruitful prognostication** sign of fertility. 58 **worky-day** ordinary. 67–73 **come . . . thee** F assigns passage to Alexas N. 68 **cannot go** cannot walk (cannot be pregnant?) **Isis** N. 76 **loose-wiv'd** married to a wanton.

6

Alexas. Lo, now, if it lay in their hands to make me
a cuckold, they would make themselves whores, but
they'ld do't.   82

Enter Cleopatra.

Enobarbus. Hush! here comes Antony.
Charmian.   Not he, the queen.
Cleopatra. Saw you my lord?
Enobarbus.   No, lady.
Cleopatra.   Was he not here?
Charmian. No, madam.
Cleopatra. He was dispos'd to mirth, but on the
    sudden   86
A Roman thought hath struck him. Enobarbus!
Enobarbus. Madam?
Cleopatra. Seek him, and bring him hither. Where's
    Alexas?   89
Alexas. Here, at your service. My lord approaches.

Enter Antony, with a Messenger [and Attendants].

Cleopatra. We will not look upon him. Go with us.
        *Exeunt [Cleopatra, Enobarbus, Alexas, Iras,
            Charmian, Soothsayer, and Attendants].*
Messenger. Fulvia thy wife first came into the field.
Antony. Against my brother Lucius?
Messenger. Ay: 94
But soon that war had end, and the time's state
Made friends of them, jointing their force 'gainst
    Caesar,
Whose better issue in the war from Italy   97

84 Saw F *saue.* 87 **A Roman thought** thought inspired by Roman
virtue. 95 **time's state** situation at that moment. 96 **jointing**
uniting (cf. *Cymbeline*, V.4.143, *jointed*). 97 **issue** success.

Upon the first encounter drave them.

Antony.   Well, what worst?

Messenger. The nature of bad news infects the teller.

Antony. When it concerns the fool, or coward. On.
Things that are past are done with me. 'Tis thus:
Who tells me true, though in his tale lie death,
I hear him as he flatter'd.

Messenger.   Labienus—   103
This is stiff news—hath with his Parthian force
Extended Asia: from Euphrates his conquering
Banner shook from Syria to Lydia   106
And to Ionia, whilst—

Antony.   Antony, thou wouldst say.

Messenger. O, my lord.

Antony.   Speak to me home.   108
Mince not the general tongue, name
Cleopatra as she is call'd in Rome:
Rail thou in Fulvia's phrase, and taunt my faults
With such full license as both truth and malice   112
Have power to utter. O, then we bring forth weeds
When our quick minds lie still, and our ills told us
Is as our earing. Fare thee well awhile.

Messenger. At your noble pleasure.   116

                                        Exit Messenger.

Antony. From Sicyon, ho, the news! Speak there!

1. Attendant. The man from Sicyon, is there such
          an one?

103 as as if. Labienus N. 105–8 Extended . . . lord N. 105 Extended taken possession of. 106 Lydia N. 108 home plainly.
109 Mince extenuate. general tongue common report. 114 minds
F *windes*. 114–15 our ills . . . earing N. 115 earing ploughing.
SD Exit Messenger F reads 'Enter another Messenger' after
this direction. 117 ho F *how*. 118 1. Attendant F. *1. Mess.*

8

2. Attendant. He stays upon your will.
Antony.   Let him appear.
These strong Egyptian fetters I must break,   120
Or lose myself in dotage.

Enter another Messenger, with a letter.

                              What are you?
2. Messenger. Fulvia thy wife is dead.
Antony.   Where died she?
2. Messenger. In Sicyon:
Her length of sickness, with what else more serious
Importeth thee to know, this bears.   125
                              [*Gives a letter.*]
Antony. Forbear me.   [*Exit 2. Messenger.*]
There's a great spirit gone! Thus did I desire it:
What our contempts doth often hurl from us   128
We wish it ours again. The present pleasure,
By revolution low'ring, does become
The opposite of itself: she's good, being gone;
The hand could pluck her back that shov'd her on.
I must from this enchanting queen break off: 133
Ten thousand harms, more than the ills I know,
My idleness doth hatch.

Enter Enobarbus.

                              How now, Enobarbus!
Enobarbus. What's your pleasure, sir?   136
Antony. I must with haste from hence.
Enobarbus. Why, then, we kill all our women. We

119 2. Attendant F *2. Mess.* stays upon your will awaits your
command. 121 lose myself become lost. 122 **2. Messenger F**
3. Mess. 125 Importeth concerns. 126 **Forbear me** leave me.
130 By . . . low'ring N. 135 **idleness** trifling, dotage.

9

see how mortal an unkindness is to them; if they
suffer our departure death's the word. 140

Antony. I must be gone.

Enobarbus. Under a compelling occasion let women
die. It were pity to cast them away for nothing,
though between them and a great cause they should
be esteemed nothing. Cleopatra, catching but the
least noise of this, dies instantly: I have seen her die
twenty times upon far poorer moment. I do think
there is mettle in death which commits some loving
act upon her, she hath such a celerity in dying. 149

Antony. She is cunning past man's thought.

Enobarbus. Alack, sir, no; her passions are made
of nothing but the finest part of pure love. We cannot call her winds and waters sighs and tears: they
are greater storms and tempests than almanacs can
report. This cannot be cunning in her; if it be, she
makes a shower of rain as well as Jove. 156

Antony. Would I had never seen her!

Enobarbus. O, sir, you had then left unseen a
wonderful piece of work which not to have been
blessed withal would have discredited your travel.

Antony. Fulvia is dead. 161

Enobarbus. Sir?

Antony. Fulvia is dead.

Enobarbus. Fulvia!

Antony. Dead. 165

Enobarbus. Why, sir, give the gods a thankful
sacrifice: when it pleaseth their deities to take the
wife of a man from him, it shows to man the tailors

142 **a compelling occasion** F *a compelling an occasion.* 146 **noise**
rumor. 147 **poorer moment** less cause. 148 **mettle** vigor. 156 **Jove**
Jupiter Pluvius, the rain god of the Romans. 168–9 **tailors of the
earth** the gods.

of the earth: comforting therein, that when old robes
are worn out there are members to make new. If
there were no more women but Fulvia, then had you
indeed a cut, and the case to be lamented. This grief
is crown'd with consolation; your old smock brings
forth a new petticoat, and indeed the tears live in an
onion that should water this sorrow.   175

Antony. The business she hath broached in the state
Cannot endure my absence.

Enobarbus. And the business you have broach'd
here cannot be without you, especially that of Cleopatra's, which wholly depends on your abode.   180

Antony. No more light answers. Let our officers
Have notice what we purpose. I shall break
The cause of our expedience to the queen,
And get her leave to part. For not alone   184
The death of Fulvia, with more urgent touches,
Do strongly speak to us, but the letters too
Of many our contriving friends in Rome
Petition us at home. Sextus Pompeius   188
Hath given the dare to Caesar, and commands
The empire of the sea. Our slippery people,
Whose love is never link'd to the deserver
Till his deserts are past, begin to throw   192
Pompey the Great and all his dignities
Upon his son, who, high in name and power,
Higher than both in blood and life, stands up
For the main soldier; whose quality going on,   196

172 **cut** blow. 176 **broached** set in motion. 180 **abode** stay. 182
break tell. 183 **expedience** haste, sudden departure. 184 **part**
depart. 185 **touches** concerns. 187 **contriving** scheming. 188 **Sextus Pompeius** N. 189 **Hath** F *Haue.* 192–4 **throw . . . Upon**
transfer. 195–6 **stands up For** aspires to be. 196 **main** foremost.
quality condition, character.

11

The sides o' th' world may danger. Much is breeding,
Which, like the courser's hair, hath yet but life,
And not a serpent's poison. Say our pleasure,
To such whose place is under us, requires   200
Our quick remove from hence.

   Enobarbus. I shall do't.   [*Exeunt.*]

   Enter Cleopatra, Charmian, Alexas, and Iras.

   Cleopatra. Where is he?
   Charmian.   I did not see him since.
   Cleopatra. See where he is, who's with him, what he
      does:
I did not send you. If you find him sad,
Say I am dancing; if in mirth, report   4
That I am sudden sick. Quick, and return.

                  [*Exit Alexas.*]

   Charmian. Madam, methinks, if you did love him
      dearly,
You do not hold the method to enforce
The like from him.
   Cleopatra.   What should I do, I do not?   8
   Charmian. In each thing give him way, cross him in
      nothing.
   Cleopatra. Thou teachest like a fool: the way to
      lose him.
   Charmian. Tempt him not so too far. I wish, for-
      bear.
In time we hate that which we often fear.   12

              Enter Antony.

197 **sides** frame. **danger** endanger. 198 **courser's hair** N. 200
place F *places.* SD **Enter Cleopatra** begins I.3. 2 **who's** F *whose.*
3 **I did not send you** let him not know I sent you. **sad** serious.
8 **I do not** that I am not doing. 11 **Tempt** test, try. **I wish, forbear**
I wish you would forbear.

But here comes Antony.

Cleopatra.　　　　　　I am sick and sullen.

Antony. I am sorry to give breathing to my pur-
　　pose.

Cleopatra. Help me away, dear Charmian, I shall
　　fall.
It cannot be thus long, the sides of nature　　　16
Will not sustain it.

Antony.　　　　　Now, my dearest queen—

Cleopatra. Pray you, stand farther from me.

Antony.　　　　　　　What's the matter?

Cleopatra. I know by that same eye there's some
　　good news.
What says the married woman? You may go.　　20
Would she had never given you leave to come!
Let her not say 'tis I that keep you here,
I have no power upon you: hers you are.

Antony. The gods best know—

Cleopatra.　　　　　O, never was there queen
So mightily betray'd: yet at the first　　　25
I saw the treasons planted.

Antony.　　　　　Cleopatra—

Cleopatra. Why should I think you can be mine and
　　true,
(Though you in swearing shake the throned gods)
Who have been false to Fulvia? Riotous madness,
To be entangled with those mouth-made vows,　　30
Which break themselves in swearing.

Antony.　　　　　　Most sweet queen—

Cleopatra. Nay, pray you, seek no color for your
　　going,　　　32

14 breathing utterance. 16 sides of nature human frame. 20 married woman Fulvia. woman? You may go. F *woman you may go?*
32 color pretext.

13

But bid farewell, and go: when you su'd staying
Then was the time for words: no going then,
Eternity was in our lips and eyes, 35
Bliss in our brows' bent: none our parts so poor
But was a race of heaven. They are so still,
Or thou, the greatest soldier of the world,
Art turn'd the greatest liar.
   Antony.   How now, lady?
   Cleopatra. I would I had thy inches; thou shouldst
     know 40
There were a heart in Egypt.
   Antony.   Hear me, queen:
The strong necessity of time commands
Our services awhile, but my full heart
Remains in use with you. Our Italy 44
Shines o'er with civil swords; Sextus Pompeius
Makes his approaches to the port of Rome;
Equality of two domestic powers
Breed scrupulous faction: the hated, grown to
     strength, 48
Are newly grown to love: the condemn'd Pompey,
Rich in his father's honor, creeps apace
Into the hearts of such as have not thriv'd
Upon the present state, whose numbers threaten;
And quietness, grown sick of rest, would purge 53
By any desperate change. My more particular,

33 **su'd staying** begged to stay. 36 **brows' bent** arch of the eye-
brows. **none our parts** none of our parts. 37 **race of heaven** of
heavenly flavor. 41 **heart in Egypt** heart (courage) in Cleopatra.
44 **in use with you** yours to keep and enjoy. 45 **civil swords**
swords drawn in civil war. 48 **scrupulous faction** quarrel over
small differences. 49 **condemn'd** stressed —'—. 52 **state** government. 53–4 **grown . . . change** N. 54 **particular** personal concern.
   14

And that which most with you should safe my going,
Is Fulvia's death.   56

   Cleopatra. Though age from folly could not give
     me freedom,
It does from childishness. Can Fulvia die?

   Antony. She's dead, my queen.
Look here, and at thy sovereign leisure read   60
The garboils she awak'd: at the last, best,
See when and where she died.

   Cleopatra.   O most false love!
Where be the sacred vials thou shouldst fill
With sorrowful water? Now I see, I see,   64
In Fulvia's death, how mine receiv'd shall be.

   Antony. Quarrel no more, but be prepar'd to know
The purposes I bear: which are or cease
As you shall give th' advice. By the fire   68
That quickens Nilus' slime, I go from hence
Thy soldier, servant, making peace or war
As thou affects.

   Cleopatra.   Cut my lace, Charmian, come,
But let it be, I am quickly ill, and well—   72
So Antony loves.

   Antony.   My precious queen, forbear,
And give true evidence to his love which stands
An honorable trial.

   Cleopatra.   So Fulvia told me.
I prithee, turn aside and weep for her,   76
Then bid adieu to me, and say the tears
Belong to Egypt. Good now, play one scene
Of excellent dissembling, and let it look   79

55 **safe** make safe. 61 **garboils** brawls. **at the last, best** the last
and best news. 63 **sacred vials** N. 67 **are** exist. 68–9 **By the fire**
. . . **slime** N. 71 **lace** lace of her bodice. 73 **So** provided. 74 **his**
love which the love of one who. 75 **told me** taught me.

Like perfect honor.

Antony.   You'll heat my blood; no more.

Cleopatra. You can do better yet: but this is
     meetly.

Antony. Now, by my sword—

Cleopatra.   And target. Still he mends.
But this is not the best. Look, prithee, Charmian
How this Herculean Roman does become   84
The carriage of his chafe.

Antony.   I'll leave you, lady.

Cleopatra. Courteous lord, one word:
Sir, you and I must part, but that's not it:
Sir, you and I have lov'd, but there's not it: 88
That you know well: something it is I would—
O, my oblivion is a very Antony,
And I am all forgotten.

Antony.   But that your royalty
Holds idleness your subject, I should take you   92
For idleness itself.

Cleopatra.   'Tis sweating labor
To bear such idleness so near the heart
As Cleopatra this. But, sir, forgive me,
Since my becomings kill me when they do not   96
Eye well to you. Your honor calls you hence;
Therefore be deaf to my unpitied folly,
And all the gods go with you. Upon your sword
Sit laurel victory, and smooth success   100
Be strew'd before your feet!

Antony.   Let us go.
Come. Our separation so abides and flies,

81 **meetly** fairly good. 82 **by my sword** F *by sword*. **target** shield.
84–5 **How . . . chafe** N. 90–1 **O . . . forgotten** N. 91 **But that**
if it were not that. 92 **idleness** frivolousness. 96 **becomings** graces.
97 **Eye well** appear well.

That thou residing here, goes yet with me
And I hence fleeting here remain with thee.   104
Away!   *Exeunt.*

Enter Octavius [Caesar], reading a letter,
Lepidus, and their train.

Caesar. You may see, Lepidus, and henceforth
      know,
It is not Caesar's natural vice to hate
Our great competitor. From Alexandria
This is the news: he fishes, drinks, and wastes   4
The lamps of night in revel: is not more manlike
Than Cleopatra, nor the queen of Ptolemy
More womanly than he. Hardly gave audience
Or vouchsaf'd to think he had partners. You   8
Shall find there a man who is th' abstract of all faults,
That all men follow.
Lepidus.   I must not think
There are evils enow to darken all his goodness:
His faults in him seem as the spots of heaven,   12
More fiery by night's blackness; hereditary
Rather than purchas'd: what he cannot change
Than what he chooses.   15
Caesar. You are too indulgent. Let's grant it is not
Amiss to tumble on the bed of Ptolemy,
To give a kingdom for a mirth, to sit
And keep the turn of tippling with a slave,
To reel the streets at noon, and stand the buffet 20

SD **Enter Octavius** begins I.4. 3 **Our** F *One.* **competitor** associate.
6 **queen of Ptolemy** N. 7–11 **More . . . goodness** N. 8 **vouchsaf'd**
F *vouchsafe.* 9 **abstract** epitome; F *abstracts.* 11 **enow** enough.
14 **purchas'd** acquired. 18 **mirth** entertainment. 19 **keep the turn
of** take turns. 20–1 **stand . . . knaves** condescend to exchange
blows with the riffraff.

17

With knaves that smells of sweat. Say this becomes him
(As his composure must be rare indeed
Whom these things cannot blemish)—yet must Antony
No way excuse his foils, when we do bear   24
So great weight in his lightness. If he fill'd
His vacancy with his voluptuousness,
Full surfeits and the dryness of his bones
Call on him for't. But to confound such time   28
That drums him from his sport, and speaks as loud
As his own state and ours, 'tis to be chid
As we rate boys who, being mature in knowledge,
Pawn their experience to their present pleasure,   32
And so rebel to judgment.

Enter a Messenger.

Lepidus.   Here's more news.
Messenger. Thy biddings have been done, and every hour,
Most noble Caesar, shalt thou have report
How 'tis abroad. Pompey is strong at sea,   36
And it appears he is belov'd of those
That only have fear'd Caesar: to the ports
The discontents repair, and men's reports   39

21 **smells** old plural form in *s* is common in Shakespeare; see
l. 48 below. 22 **composure** disposition. 24 **foils** disgraces N. 24-5
when . . . lightness when his levity affects us so seriously. 26
vacancy leisure. 28 **Call on** call to account. **confound** put to ill
use. 29 **drums** calls as drum calls to battle. 29-30 **speaks . . .
ours** speaks of weighty matters of triumvirate. 31 **rate** scold.
mature in knowledge old enough to know. 32 **Pawn . . . pleasure**
gratify their desires against their judgment. 39 **discontents** discontented.

18

Give him much wrong'd.

Caesar.   I should have known no less.
It hath bin taught us from the primal state
That he which is was wish'd until he were;
And the ebb'd man, ne're lov'd till ne're worth love,
Comes dear'd by being lack'd. This common body,   45
Like to a vagabond flag upon the stream,
Goes to and back, lacking the varying tide,
To rot itself with motion.

Messenger.   Caesar, I bring thee word,
Menecrates and Menas, famous pirates,   48
Makes the sea serve them, which they ear and wound
With keels of every kind. Many hot inroads
They make in Italy; the borders maritime   51
Lack blood to think on't, and flush youth revolt;
No vessel can peep forth, but 'tis as soon
Taken as seen: for Pompey's name strikes more
Than could his war resisted.

Caesar.   Antony,
Leave thy lascivious wassails. When thou once   56
Was beaten from Modena, where thou slew'st
Hirsius and Pansa, consuls, at thy heel
Did famine follow, whom thou fought'st against,
(Though daintily brought up) with patience more
Than savages could suffer. Thou didst drink   61
The stale of horses and the gilded puddle
Which beasts would cough at: thy palate then did
          deign

40 **Give him** represent him as. 41 **bin** been. **primal** primeval.
43 **ebb'd** declined in fortune. **ne're** ne'er. 44 **Comes dear'd** F
Comes fear'd. 45 **vagabond** shifty. **flag** iris. 46 **lacking** lackeying,
following like a lackey. 49 **ear** plough. 52 **Lack blood** turn pale.
flush vigorous. 54–5 **strikes . . . resisted** N. 56 **wassails** revels.
56–71 **When . . . lank'd** not N. 62 **stale** urine. **gilded** of a golden
color.

The roughest berry on the rudest hedge;   64
Yea, like the stag, when snow the pasture sheets,
The barks of trees thou brows'd. On the Alps
It is reported thou didst eat strange flesh,
Which some did die to look on. And all this—   68
(It wounds thine honor that I speak it now)—
Was borne so like a soldier that thy cheek
So much as lank'd not.

   Lepidus.   'Tis pity of him.

   Caesar. Let his shames quickly   72
Drive him to Rome. 'Tis time we twain
Did show ourselves i' th' field, and to that end
Assemble we immediate council. Pompey
Thrives in our idleness.

   Lepidus.   Tomorrow, Caesar,   76
I shall be furnish'd to inform you rightly
Both what by sea and land I can be able
To front this present time.

   Caesar.   Till which encounter,
It is my business too. Farewell.   80

   Lepidus. Farewell, my lord. What you shall know
      meantime
Of stirs abroad, I shall beseech you, sir,
To let me be partaker.

   Caesar.   Doubt not, sir;   83
I knew it for my bond.   *Exeunt.*

   Enter Cleopatra, Charmian, Iras, and Mardian.

   Cleopatra. Charmian!
   Charmian. Madam?

66 **brows'd** browsed'st. 71 **lank'd** not did not grow thin. 75 **we**
F *me.* 78 **can be able** can muster. 79 **front** face. 84 **bond** duty,
obligation. SD **Enter Cleopatra** begins I.5.

Cleopatra. Ha, ha! Give me to drink mandragora.
Charmian. Why, madam?   4
Cleopatra. That I might sleep out this great gap of
    time
My Antony is away.
Charmian.   You think of him too much.
Cleopatra. O! 'tis treason.
Charmian.   Madam, I trust, not so.
Cleopatra. Thou, eunuch Mardian.
Mardian.   What's your highness' pleasure?
Cleopatra. Not now to hear thee sing. I take no
    pleasure   9
In aught an eunuch has. 'Tis well for thee,
That, being unseminar'd, thy freer thoughts
May not fly forth of Egypt. Hast thou affections?
Mardian. Yes, gracious madam.   13
Cleopatra. Indeed?
Mardian. Not in deed, madam, for I can do nothing
But what indeed is honest to be done: 16
Yet have I fierce affections, and think
What Venus did with Mars.
Cleopatra.   O Charmian,
Where think'st thou he is now? Stands he, or sits he?
Or does he walk? or is he on his horse?   20
O happy horse, to bear the weight of Antony!
Do bravely, horse, for wot'st thou whom thou mov'st?
The demi-Atlas of this earth, the arm
And burgonet of men. He's speaking now,   24
Or murmuring 'Where's my serpent of old Nile?'
(For so he calls me). Now I feed myself
With most delicious poison. Think on me,

3 **mandragora** mandrake, a narcotic. 11 **unseminar'd** unsexed.
12 **affections** passions. 22 **wot'st** knowest. 23 **demi-Atlas** N. 24
burgonet helmet.

21

That am with Phoebus' amorous pinches black,   28
And wrinkled deep in time? Broad-fronted Caesar,
When thou wast here above the ground, I was
A morsel for a monarch, and great Pompey
Would stand and make his eyes grow in my brow;
There would he anchor his aspect and die   33
With looking on his life.

Enter Alexas from Antony.

Alexas.   Sovereign of Egypt, hail!
Cleopatra. How much unlike art thou Mark Antony!
Yet, coming from him, that great med'cine hath
With his tinct gilded thee.   37
How goes it with my brave Mark Antony?
Alexas. Last thing he did, dear queen,
He kiss'd—the last of many doubled kisses—   40
This orient pearl. His speech sticks in my heart.
Cleopatra. Mine ear must pluck it thence.
Alexas.   'Good friend,' quoth he,
'Say, the firm Roman to great Egypt sends
This treasure of an oyster; at whose foot,   44
To mend the petty present, I will piece
Her opulent throne with kingdoms. All the East,
(Say thou) shall call her mistress.' So he nodded,
And soberly did mount an arm-gaunt steed,   48
Who neigh'd so high that what I would have spoke
Was beastly dumb'd by him.
Cleopatra.   What was he, sad or merry?

29 **Broad-fronted** with broad forehead. 31 **great Pompey** N. 33 **aspect** look (stressed — —′). SD **Antony** F *Caesar*. 36 **that great med'cine** N. 37 **tinct** tincture, color. 38 **brave** splendid. 43 **firm** constant. 45 **mend** improve. **piece** piece out. 48 **arm-gaunt** worn thin with hard campaign service. 50 **dumb'd** silenced; F *dumbe*.

22

Alexas. Like to the time o' th' year between the
    extremes
Of hot and cold, he was nor sad nor merry.   52
  Cleopatra. O well-divided disposition! Note him,
Note him, good Charmian, 'tis the man; but note him.
He was not sad, for he would shine on those   55
That make their looks by his. He was not merry,
Which seem'd to tell them his remembrance lay
In Egypt with his joy; but between both.
O heavenly mingle! Be'st thou sad or merry,
The violence of either thee becomes,   60
So does it no man else. Met'st thou my posts?
  Alexas. Ay, madam, twenty several messengers.
Why do you send so thick?
  Cleopatra.   Who's born that day
When I forget to send to Antony,   64
Shall die a beggar. Ink and paper, Charmian.
Welcome, my good Alexas. Did I, Charmian,
Ever love Caesar so?
  Charmian.   O, that brave Caesar.   67
  Cleopatra. Be chok'd with such another emphasis!
Say, the brave Antony.
  Charmian.   The valiant Caesar!
  Cleopatra. By Isis, I will give thee bloody teeth,
If thou with Caesar paragon again   71
My man of men.
  Charmian.   By your most gracious pardon,
I sing but after you.
  Cleopatra.   My salad days,
When I was green in judgment, cold in blood,
To say as I said then. But come, away,

53 disposition mood. 54 **the man** the very man. 61 **posts** messengers. 63 **thick** in quick succession. 71 **paragon** compare. 73 **salad
days** inexperienced youth.

Get me ink and paper.   76
He shall have every day a several greeting,
Or I'll unpeople Egypt.   *Exeunt.*

Enter Pompey, Menecrates, and Menas, in
warlike manner.

Pompey. If the great gods be just, they shall assist
The deeds of justest men.
    Menecrates.   Know, worthy Pompey,
That what they do delay, they not deny.
    Pompey. Whiles we are suitors to their throne,
        decays   4
The thing we sue for.
    Menecrates.   We, ignorant of ourselves,
Beg often our own harms, which the wise powers
Deny us for our good: so find we profit
By losing of our prayers.
    Pompey.   I shall do well: 8
The people love me, and the sea is mine;
My powers are crescent, and my auguring hope
Says it will come to th' full. Mark Antony
In Egypt sits at dinner, and will make   12
No wars without doors. Caesar gets money where
He loses hearts: Lepidus flatters both,
Of both is flatter'd: but he neither loves,
Nor either cares for him.   16
    Menas. Caesar and Lepidus are in the field.
A mighty strength they carry.
    Pompey. Where have you this? 'Tis false.
    Menas.   From Silvius, sir.

SD Enter Pompey begins II.1. 2–5 Know . . . for N. 2 worthy
noble. 6 powers forces. 10 crescent growing. auguring prophesy-
ing. 17, 19, 39 Menas F *Mene;* see Appendix A, 2.
    24

Pompey. He dreams: I know they are in Rome to-
gether,   20
Looking for Antony. But all the charms of love,
Salt Cleopatra, soften thy wan'd lip!
Let witchcraft join with beauty, lust with both!
Tie up the libertine in a field of feasts,   24
Keep his brain fuming; Epicurean cooks
Sharpen with cloyless sauce his appetite,
That sleep and feeding may prorogue his honor   27
Even till a Lethe'd dullness—

Enter Varrius.

How now, Varrius!
Varrius. This is most certain that I shall deliver:
Mark Antony is every hour in Rome
Expected. Since he went from Egypt 'tis   31
A space for farther travel.
Pompey.   I could have given less matter
A better ear. Menas, I did not think
This amorous surfeiter would have donn'd his helm
For such a petty war: his soldiership
Is twice the other twain. But let us rear   36
The higher our opinion, that our stirring
Can from the lap of Egypt's widow pluck
The ne're lust-wearied Antony.
Menas.   I cannot hope
Caesar and Antony shall well greet together;   40

22 Salt lustful. wan'd faded. 26 cloyless which will not satiate.
27–8 prorogue . . . dullness suspend completely his sense of
honor. 28 Lethe'd N. 29 that what. deliver report. 31–2 'tis . . .
travel there has been time for a longer journey. 36–7 rear . . .
opinion prize ourselves more highly. 38 Egypt's widow Cleopatra,
young King Ptolemy's widow. 39 hope suppose. 40 greet together commune amicably.

25

His wife that's dead did trespasses to Caesar,
His brother warr'd upon him, although I think
Not mov'd by Antony.

   Pompey.   I know not, Menas,
How lesser enmities may give way to greater.   **44**
Were't not that we stand up against them all,
'Twere pregnant they should square between them-
      selves,
For they have entertained cause enough
To draw their swords: but how the fear of us   **48**
May ciment their divisions and bind up
The petty difference, we yet not know.
Be't as our gods will have't! It only stands
Our lives upon, to use our strongest hands.   **52**
Come, Menas.   *Exeunt.*

        Enter Enobarbus and Lepidus.

   Lepidus. Good Enobarbus, 'tis a worthy deed,
And shall become you well, to entreat your captain
To soft and gentle speech.

   Enobarbus.   I shall entreat him
To answer like himself: if Caesar move him,   **4**
Let Antony look over Caesar's head,
And speak as loud as Mars. By Jupiter,
Were I the wearer of Antonio's beard,
I would not shave't today.   **8**

   Lepidus. 'Tis not a time for private stomaching.

---

42 His brother Lucius Antonius N. **warr'd** F *wan'd.* **46 pregnant**
very probable. **square** quarrel. **49 ciment** cement (stressed —' —).
51–2 It only . . . upon N. SD **Enter Enobarbus** begins II.2.
2 to entreat read 't'entreat.' **4 like himself** as befits his character.
8 would not shave't would dare him (Caesar) to pluck it N.
9 stomaching resentment.

Enobarbus. Every time serves for the matter that
is then born in't.
Lepidus. But small to greater matters must give
way.
Enobarbus. Not if the small come first.   12
Lepidus. Your speech is passion: but pray you stir
No embers up. Here comes the noble Antony.

Enter Antony and Ventidius.

Enobarbus. And yonder, Caesar.

Enter Caesar, Maecenas, and Agrippa.

Antony. If we compose well here, to Parthia: 16
Hark, Ventidius.
Caesar. I do not know, Maecenas; ask Agrippa.
Lepidus. Noble friends:
That which combin'd us was most great, and let not
A leaner action rend us. What's amiss,   21
May it be gently heard. When we debate
Our trivial difference loud, we do commit
Murther in healing wounds. Then, noble partners,
The rather for I earnestly beseech,   25
Touch you the sourest points with sweetest terms,
Nor curstness grow to th' matter.
Antony.   'Tis spoken well.
Were we before our armies, and to fight,   28
I should do thus.   *Flourish.*
Caesar. Welcome to Rome.
Antony.   Thank you.
Caesar.   Sit.
Antony.   Sit, sir.

16 **compose** come to an agreement. 17 **Hark** F *Hearke* N. 27
curstness ill humor. **grow to** be added to.

Caesar.   Nay, then.

Antony. I learn, you take things ill which are not
      30:

Or being, concern you not.

Caesar.   I must be laugh'd at

If, or for nothing or a little, I   33

Should say myself offended, and with you

Chiefly i' th' world; more laugh'd at that I should

Once name you derogately, when to sound your name

It not concern'd me.   37

   Antony. My being in Egypt, Caesar, what was't to
      you?

   Caesar. No more than my residing here at Rome

Might be to you in Egypt: yet, if you there   40

Did practice on my state, your being in Egypt

Might be my question.

   Antony.   How intend you, practic'd?

   Caesar. You may be pleas'd to catch at mine intent

By what did here befall me. Your wife and brother

Made wars upon me, and their contestation   45

Was theme for you, you were the word of war.

   Antony. You do mistake your business; my brother
      never

Did urge me in his act: I did inquire it,   48

And have my learning from some true reports

That drew their swords with you. Did he not rather

Discredit my authority with yours,

And make the wars alike against my stomach,   52

Having alike your cause? Of this my letters

33 or . . . or either . . . or. 36 **derogately** disparagingly. **sound**
mention. 41 **practice on** plot against. 42 **question** concern. **intend**
mean. 46 **Was theme for you** was undertaken in your behalf and
interest. **word** watchword. 48 **urge me** use my name. 49 **reports**
reporters. 52 **stomach** desire. 53 **Having . . . cause** since I had
the same cause as you (to be displeased with him).

Before did satisfy you. If you'll patch a quarrel,
As matter whole you have to make it with,
It must not be with this.

Caesar.   You praise yourself   56
By laying defects of judgment to me, but
You patch'd up your excuses.

  Antony.   Not so, not so;
I know you could not lack, I am certain on't,
Very necessity of this thought, that I,   60
Your partner in the cause 'gainst which he fought,
Could not with graceful eyes attend those wars
Which fronted mine own peace. As for my wife,
I would you had her spirit in such another: 64
The third o' th' world is yours, which with a snaffle
You may pace easy, but not such a wife.

Enobarbus. Would we had all such wives, that the
men might go to wars with the women!   68

Antony. So much uncurbable, her garboils, Caesar,
Made out of her impatience—which not wanted
Shrodenesse of policy too—I grieving grant
Did you too much disquiet; for that you must   72
But say I could not help it.

Caesar.   I wrote to you:
When rioting in Alexandria you
Did pocket up my letters, and with taunts
Did gibe my missive out of audience.

  Antony.   Sir,   76
He fell upon me, ere admitted, then:
Three kings I had newly feasted, and did want

54 **patch** make out of, i.e. start a quarrel. 55 **you have to** N. 62
graceful . . . attend regard favorably. 63 **fronted** opposed. 65
snaffle bridle bit. 66 **pace easy** control easily. 69 **garboils** disturbances. 71 **Shrodenesse** shrewdness. 76 **missive** messenger.
78 **I had** read 'I'd.' 78–9 **did want . . . morning** lacked mastery
of myself which I had possessed in the morning.

Of what I was i' th' morning; but next day
I told him of myself, which was as much   80
As to have ask'd him pardon. Let this fellow
Be nothing of our strife: if we contend,
Out of our question wipe him.

Caesar.   You have broken
The article of your oath, which you shall never   84
Have tongue to charge me with.

Lepidus.   Soft, Caesar.

Antony. No, Lepidus, let him speak.
The honor is sacred which he talks on now,
Supposing that I lack'd it. But on, Caesar,   88
The article of my oath—

Caesar. To lend me arms and aid when I requir'd
      them
The which you both denied.

Antony.   Neglected, rather: 91
And then when poison'd hours had bound me up
From mine own knowledge. As nearly as I may,
I'll play the penitent to you. But mine honesty
Shall not make poor my greatness, nor my power
Work without it. Truth is that Fulvia,   96
To have me out of Egypt, made wars here;
For which myself, the ignorant motive, do
So far ask pardon as befits mine honor
To stoop in such a case.

Lepidus.   'Tis noble spoken.   100

Maecenas. If it might please you, to enforce no
      further
The griefs between ye: to forget them quite

---

80 **told him of myself** explained my condition to him. 82 **nothing of**
irrelevant to. 83 **question** debate. 87–8 **The honor . . . it** N.
93 **From mine own knowledge** (kept me) from knowing what I
was doing. 94–6 **But . . . without it** N. 96–7 **Fulvia . . . here** N.
102 **griefs** grievances.

Were to remember that the present need   108
Speaks to atone you.
 Lepidus.   Worthily spoken, Maecenas.
 Enobarbus. Or, if you borrow one another's love for
the instant, you may, when you hear no more words
of Pompey, return it again: you shall have time to
wrangle in when you have nothing else to do.   108
 Antony. Thou art a soldier only; speak no more.
 Enobarbus. That truth should be silent I had al-
most forgot.
 Antony. You wrong this presence; therefore speak
no more.   113
 Enobarbus. Go to, then; your considerate stone.
 Caesar. I do not much dislike the matter, but
The manner of his speech: for't cannot be   116
We shall remain in friendship, our conditions
So diff'ring in their acts. Yet, if I knew
What hoop should hold us staunch, from edge to
  edge
O' th' world I would pursue it.   120
 Agrippa. Give me leave, Caesar.
 Caesar.   Speak, Agrippa.
 Agrippa. Thou hast a sister by the mother's side,
Admir'd Octavia; great Mark Antony
Is now a widower.
 Caesar. Say not so, Agrippa: 124
If Cleopatra heard you, your reproof
Were well deserv'd of rashness.

---

104 atone reconcile. Worthily nobly. 113 presence august company. 114 Go to, then very well. considerate stone I will think
but remain dumb as a stone. 117 conditions dispositions. 122 by
the mother's side N. 124 not so, F *not, say.* 125 reproof F
proofe. 126 deserv'd of rashness deserved because of your
rashness (in speaking as you do).

Antony. I am not married, Caesar: let me hear
Agrippa further speak.   128

Agrippa. To hold you in perpetual amity,
To make you brothers, and to knit your hearts
With an unslipping knot, take Antony
Octavia to his wife: whose beauty claims   132
No worse a husband than the best of men: whose
Virtue and whose general graces speak
That which none else can utter. By this marriage,
All little jealousies which now seem great,   136
And all great fears, which now import their dangers,
Would then be nothing. Truths would be tales,
Where now half tales be truths: her love to both
Would each to other and all loves to both   140
Draw after her. Pardon what I have spoke,
For 'tis a studied, not a present thought,
By duty ruminated.

Antony.   Will Caesar speak?   143

Caesar. Not till he hears how Antony is touch'd
With what is spoke already.

Antony.   What power is in Agrippa,
If I would say, 'Agrippa, be it so,'
To make this good?

Caesar.   The power of Caesar,
And his power unto Octavia.

Antony.   May I never   148
To this good purpose that so fairly shows
Dream of impediment! Let me have thy hand;
Further this act of grace, and from this hour
The heart of brothers govern in our loves   152
And sway our great designs.

---

136 jealousies suspicions. 137 **import** carry with them. 138–9
Truths . . . truths N. 142 **present** sudden. 149 **so fairly shows**
looks so promising.

Caesar.   There's my hand.
A sister I bequeath you, whom no brother
Did ever love so dearly. Let her live
To join our kingdoms and our hearts, and never
Fly off our loves again.
   Lepidus.   Happily, amen.   157
   Antony. I did not think to draw my sword 'gainst
        Pompey,
For he hath laid strange courtesies and great
Of late upon me. I must thank him only,   159
Lest my remembrance suffer ill report;
At heel of that, defy him.
   Lepidus.   Time calls upon's.
Of us must Pompey presently be sought,
Or else he seeks out us.
   Antony.   Where lies he?   164
   Caesar. About the Mount Mesena.
   Antony. What is his strength by land?
   Caesar. Great and increasing:
But by sea he is an absolute master.   168
   Antony. So is the fame.
Would we had spoke together! Haste we for it:
Yet, ere we put ourselves in arms, dispatch we
The business we have talk'd of.
   Caesar.   With most gladness;
And do invite you to my sister's view,   173
Whither straight I'll lead you.
   Antony. Let us, Lepidus, not lack your company.
   Lepidus. Noble Antony, not sickness should detain
        me.   *Flourish. Exit omnes. Mane[n]t*
                    Enobarbus, Agrippa, Maecenas.

159 strange rare. 161 remembrance memory of favors shown.
163 Of by. presently immediately. 165 Mesena Misenum, a
harbor in southern Italy. 169 fame rumor. 172 most greatest.
173 do I do.

Maecenas. Welcome from Egypt, sir. 177

Enobarbus. Half the heart of Caesar, worthy Maecenas. My honourable friend, Agrippa.

Agrippa. Good Enobarbus. 180

Maecenas. We have cause to be glad that matters are so well disgested. You stayed well by't in Egypt.

Enobarbus. Ay, sir, we did sleep day out of countenance, and made the night light with drinking. 184

Maecenas. Eight wild boars roasted whole at a breakfast: and but twelve persons there. Is this true?

Enobarbus. This was but as a fly by an eagle: we had much more monstrous matter of feast, which worthily deserved noting. 189

Maecenas. She's a most triumphant lady, if report be square to her.

Enobarbus. When she first met Mark Antony, she purs'd up his heart, upon the river of Cydnus. 193

Agrippa. There she appear'd indeed, or my reporter devis'd well for her.

Enobarbus. I will tell you. 196
The barge she sat in, like a burnish'd throne
Burnt on the water: the poop was beaten gold,
Purple the sails, and so perfumed that
The winds were lovesick with them; the oars were
    silver, 200
Which to the tune of flutes kept stroke, and made
The water which they beat to follow faster,
As amorous of their strokes. For her own person,
It beggar'd all description; she did lie 204

178 **Half . . . Caesar** N. 182 **disgested** digested. **stayed well by't**
kept it up. 185 **Eight wild boars** N. 187 **by** in comparison with.
190 **triumphant** magnificent. 191 **square** just, fair. 193 **purs'd up**
pocketed. **Cydnus** F *Sidnis*; V.2.231, *Cidrus*. 195 **devis'd** invented. 196–224 **I will . . . nature** N. 203 **For** as for.

In her pavilion, cloth of gold of tissue,
Orepicturing that Venus where we see
The fancy outwork nature. On each side her   207
Stood pretty dimpled boys, like smiling Cupids,
With divers-color'd fans whose wind did seem
To glow the delicate cheeks which they did cool,
And what they undid did.

  Agrippa.   O, rare for Antony!

  Enobarbus. Her gentlewomen, like the Nereides,
So many mermaids tended her i' th' eyes,   213
And made their bends adornings. At the helm
A seeming mermaid steers: the silken tackle
Swell with the touches of those flower-soft hands
That yarely frame the office. From the barge   217
A strange invisible perfume hits the sense
Of the adjacent wharfs. The city cast
Her people out upon her: and Antony,   220
Enthron'd i' th' market place, did sit alone,
Whistling to th' air; which, but for vacancy,
Had gone to gaze on Cleopatra too
And made a gap in nature.

  Agrippa.   Rare Egyptian!   224

  Enobarbus. Upon her landing, Antony sent to her,
Invited her to supper: she replied,
It should be better he became her guest,
Which she entreated. Our courteous Antony,   228
Whom ne're the word of 'No' woman hard speak,
Being barber'd ten times o're, goes to the feast,

205 **cloth of gold of tissue** rich cloth interwoven with thread of gold. 206 **Orepicturing** surpassing the picture of. 207 **outwork** excel. 210 **glow** make hot; F. *gloue.* 211 **what they undid did** N. 213 **tended . . . eyes** waited upon her every wish. 214 **made . . . adornings** N. 217 **yarely** nimbly. **frame** perform. 229 **hard** heard.

And for his ordinary pays his heart
For what his eyes eat only.

    Agrippa.   Royal wench!   232
She made great Caesar lay his sword to bed;
He plough'd her, and she cropp'd.

    Enobarbus.   I saw her once
Hop forty paces through the public street;   235
And having lost her breath, she spoke, and panted
That she did make defect perfection.
And, breathless, power breathe forth.

    Maecenas. Now Antony must leave her utterly.

    Enobarbus. Never; he will not: 240
Age cannot wither her, nor custom stale
Her infinite variety: other women cloy
The appetites they feed, but she makes hungry
Where most she satisfies. For vildest things   244
Become themselves in her, that the holy priests
Bless her when she is riggish.

    Maecenas. If beauty, wisdom, modesty, can settle
The heart of Antony, Octavia is   248
A blessed lottery to him.

    Agrippa.   Let us go.
Good Enobarbus, make yourself my guest
Whilst you abide here.

    Enobarbus.   Humbly, sir, I thank you.
                              Exeunt.

Enter Antony, Caesar, Octavia between them.

    Antony. The world and my great office will some-
        times

231 ordinary dinner. 232 eat ate. 237 That so that. defect perfection she made her defective (because panting) speech perfection. 238 breathe did breathe. 241 stale make stale. 242 infinite
variety N. 244 vildest vilest. 246 riggish wanton. 249 lottery prize.
SD Enter Antony begins II.3.

Divide me from your bosom.

Octavia.   All which time
Before the gods my knee shall bow my prayers
To them for you.

Antony.   Good night, sir. My Octavia   4
Read not my blemishes in the world's report:
I have not kept my square, but that to come
Shall all be done by th' rule. Good night, dear lady.

Octavia. Good night, sir.   8

Caesar. Good night.   *Exit* [*with Octavia*].

Enter Soothsayer.

Antony. Now, sirrah; you do wish yourself in
Egypt?   11

Soothsayer. Would I had never come from thence,
nor you thither!

Antony. If you can, your reason?

Soothsayer. I see it in my motion, have it not in my
       tongue,
But yet hie you to Egypt again.   16

Antony. Say to me, whose fortunes shall rise higher,
Caesar's or mine?

Soothsayer. Caesar's.
Therefore, O Antony, stay not by his side.   20
Thy demon, that thy spirit which keeps thee, is
Noble, courageous, high, unmatchable,
Where Caesar's is not. But near him thy angel   23
Becomes a fear, as being o'repower'd; therefore
Make space enough between you.

Antony.   Speak this no more.

---

6 **square** bounds of prudence. 10 **sirrah** familiar form of 'sir,'
used sometimes contemptuously, sometimes affectionately. 15 **I
see . . . tongue** N. 21–4 **Thy demon . . . o'repower'd** N.

Soothsayer. To none but thee: no more but when to
    thee.
If thou dost play with him at any game
Thou art sure to lose; and of that natural luck   28
He beats thee 'gainst the odds. Thy luster thickens
When he shines by: I say again, thy spirit
Is all afraid to govern thee near him,
But he away, 'tis noble.

    Antony.   Get thee gone: 32
Say to Ventidius I would speak with him.

                             Exit [*Soothsayer*].
He shall to Parthia. Be it art or hap,
He hath spoken true. The very dice obey him,
And in our sports my better cunning faints   36
Under his chance; if we draw lots he speeds,
His cocks do win the battle still of mine
When it is all to nought: and his quails ever
Beat mine, inhoop'd, at odds. I will to Egypt: 40
And though I make this marriage for my peace,
I' th' east my pleasure lies. O, come Ventidius,

              Enter Ventidius.

You must to Parthia; your commission's ready:
Follow me, and receive't.   *Exeunt.*

    Enter Lepidus, Maecenas, and Agrippa.

    Lepidus. Trouble yourselves no further: pray you
    hasten
Your generals after.

27–32 If . . . 'tis noble N. 29 thickens grows dim. 30 by near by.
32 away F *alway.* 33, 42, SD Ventidius F *Ventigius;* III.1,
Ventidius. 34 art magic. hap chance. 36 better cunning superior
skill. 37 speeds is successful. 38 His cocks N. 39 When . . .
nought N. 40 inhoop'd confined in hoops. SD Enter Lepidus
begins II.4.

Agrippa.   Sir, Mark Antony
Will e'ne but kiss Octavia, and we'll follow.
Lepidus. Till I shall see you in your soldier's dress,
Which will become you both, farewell.
Maecenas.   We shall,   5
As I conceive the journey, be at Mount
Before you, Lepidus.
Lepidus.   Your way is shorter;
My purposes do draw me much about: 8
You'll win two days upon me.
Both. Sir, good success!
Lepidus. Farewell.   *Exeunt.*

Enter Cleopatra, Charmian, Iras, and Alexas.

Cleopatra. Give me some music: music, moody food
Of us that trade in love.
Attendant.   The music, ho!

Enter Mardian the eunuch.

Cleopatra. Let it alone, let's to billiards: come,
     Charmian.   3
Charmian. My arm is sore; best play with Mardian.
Cleopatra. As well a woman with an eunuch play'd
As with a woman. Come, you'll play with me, sir?
Mardian. As well as I can, madam.
Cleopatra. And when good will is show'd, though't
     come too short   8
The actor may plead pardon. I'll none now.
Give me mine angle; we'll to th' river: there,
My music playing far off, I will betray   11
Tawny-finn'd fishes; my bended hook shall pierce

6 at **Mount** at the Mount (i.e. Misenum). 8 **much about** in a
roundabout way. SD **Enter Cleopatra** begins II.5. 1 **moody** melancholy. 11 **betray** snare. 12 **Tawny-finn'd** F *Tawny fine.*

Their slimy jaws; and as I draw them up
I'll think them every one an Antony,
And say, 'Ah, ha! y'are caught.'
   Charmian.   'Twas merry when
You wager'd on your angling; when your diver   16
Did hang a salt-fish on his hook, which he
With fervency drew up.
   Cleopatra.   That time! O times!
I laugh'd him out of patience: and that night
I laugh'd him into patience, and next morn,   20
Ere the ninth hour, I drunk him to his bed;
Then put my tires and mantles on him, whilst
I wore his sword Philippan.

Enter a Messenger.

                  O, from Italy!
Ram thou thy fruitful tidings in mine ears,   24
That long time have bin barren.
   Messenger.   Madam, madam—
   Cleopatra. Antonio's dead:
If thou say so villain, thou kill'st thy mistress:
But well and free, if thou so yield him,   28
There is gold and here
My bluest veins to kiss, a hand that kings
Have lipp'd and trembl'd kissing.
   Messenger. First, madam, he is well.   32
   Cleopatra. Why, there's more gold.
But sirrah mark, we use
To say the dead are well: bring it to that,
The gold I give thee will I melt and pour   36

15–18 'Twas . . . drew up N. 22 tires head-dresses. 23 **Philippan**
N. 26–9 Antonio's . . . here N. 28 yield report. 35 well in
heaven. bring it to that say that that is your meaning.

Down thy ill-uttering throat.

Messenger. Good madam, hear me.

Cleopatra. Well, go to, I will;
But there's no goodness in thy face; if Antony
Be free and healthful, so tart a favor   40
To trumpet such good tidings! if not well,
Thou shouldst come like a Fury crown'd with snakes
Not like a formal man.

Messenger. Will't please you hear me?

Cleopatra. I have a mind to strike thee ere thou
    speak'st: 44
Yet, if thou say Antony lives, 'tis well,
Or friends with Caesar, or not captive to him,
I'll set thee in a shower of gold, and hail   47
Rich pearls upon thee.

Messenger. Madam, he's well.

Cleopatra. Well said.

Messenger. And friends with Caesar.

Cleopatra. Th'art an honest man.

Messenger. Caesar and he are greater friends than
    ever.

Cleopatra. Make thee a fortune from me.

Messenger. But yet, madam—

Cleopatra. I do not like 'but yet,' it does allay   52
The good precedence; fie upon 'but yet!'
'But yet' is as a gaoler to bring forth
Some monstrous malefactor. Prithee, friend,
Pour out the pack of matter to mine ear,   56
The good and bad together: he's friends with Caesar,
In state of health, thou say'st, and thou say'st, free.

---

40 **so tart a favor** so sour a countenance. 43 **formal** normally
shaped. 49 **honest** worthy. 53 **precedence** earlier report. 54 **gaoler**
jailer.

Messenger. Free, madam! no; I made no such report:
He's bound unto Octavia.

Cleopatra.   For what good turn?   60

Messenger. For the best turn i' th' bed.

Cleopatra.   I am pale, Charmian.

Messenger. Madam, he's married to Octavia.

Cleopatra. The most infectious pestilence upon thee!
                                        Strikes him down.

Messenger. Good madam, patience.

Cleopatra.   What say you?
                                        Strikes him.
Hence, horrible villain, or I'll spurn thine eyes   65
Like balls before me; I'll unhair thy head:
                        She hales him up and down.
Thou shalt be whipp'd with wire, and stew'd in brine,
Smarting in ling'ring pickle.

Messenger.   Gracious madam,   68
I that do bring the news made not the match.

Cleopatra. Say 'tis not so, a province I will give thee,
And make thy fortunes proud: the blow thou hadst
Shall make thy peace for moving me to rage,   72
And I will boot thee with what gift beside
Thy modesty can beg.

Messenger.   He's married, madam.

Cleopatra. Rogue, thou hast liv'd too long.
                                        Draw a knife.

Messenger.   Nay, then I'll run.
What mean you, madam? I have made no fault.   76
                                        Exit.

---

65 spurn kick. SD hales drags. 73 boot thee make amends to thee.
what whatever. 74 modesty moderation.

Charmian. Good madam, keep yourself within your-
    self;
The man is innocent.

Cleopatra. Some innocents 'scape not the thunder-
    bolt.
Melt Egypt into Nile! and kindly creatures   80
Turn all to serpents! Call the slave again:
Though I am mad, I will not bite him. Call!

Charmian. He is afeard to come.

Cleopatra.   I will not hurt him.
                                    [*Exit Charmian.*]
These hands do lack nobility, that they strike   84
A meaner than myself; since I myself
Have given myself the cause. Come hither, sir.

Enter [Charmian and] the Messenger again.

Though it be honest, it is never good
To bring bad news: give to a gracious message   88
An host of tongues, but let ill tidings tell
Themselves when they be felt.

Messenger.   I have done my duty.

Cleopatra. Is he married?
I cannot hate thee worser than I do   92
If thou again say 'Yes.'

Messenger.   He's married, madam.

Cleopatra. The gods confound thee! dost thou hold
    there still?

Messenger. Should I lie, madam?

Cleopatra.   O, I would thou didst,
So half my Egypt were submerg'd and made   96
A cesterne for scal'd snakes. Go, get thee hence;
Hadst thou Narcissus in thy face, to me

80 **kindly** benign. 88 **gracious** pleasing. 94 **confound** destroy. 96
So even though. 97 **cesterne** cistern. 98 **Narcissus** N.

Thou wouldst appear most ugly. He is married?   99
  Messenger. I crave your highness' pardon.
  Cleopatra.   He is married?
  Messenger. Take no offense that I would not offend
    you;
To punish me for what you make me do
Seems much unequal; he's married to Octavia.
  Cleopatra. O, that his fault should make a knave of
    thee,   104
That art not what th'art sure of. Get thee hence;
The marchandise which thou hast brought from
    Rome
Are all too dear for me.
Lie they upon thy hand, and be undone by 'em!   108
                                  [Exit Messenger.]

  Charmian. Good your highness, patience.
  Cleopatra. In praising Antony I have disprais'd
    Caesar.
  Charmian. Many times, madam.
  Cleopatra. I am paid for't now. Lead me from
    hence.   112
I faint. O Iras! Charmian! 'Tis no matter.
Go to the fellow, good Alexas; bid him
Report the feature of Octavia: her years,
Her inclination, let him not leave out   116
The color of her hair. Bring me word quickly.
                                    [Exit Alexas.]

Let him forever go—let him not—Charmian!
Though he be painted one way like a Gorgon,

---

101 Take . . . you N. 103 **much unequal** very unjust. 105 **That**
. . . **sure of** N. 108 **Lie . . . hand** may they remain unsold
(your merchandise). **undone** ruined. 116 **inclination** disposition.
118 **him** i.e. Antony.

The other way's a Mars. [*To Mardian.*] Bid you
    Alexas   120
Bring me word how tall she is. Pity me, Charmian,
But do not speak to me. Lead me to my chamber.
                                          Exeunt.

*Flourish. Enter Pompey at one door, with drum and
trumpet: at another Caesar, Lepidus, Antony, Enobarbus, Maecenas, Agrippa, Menas, with Soldiers
marching.*

  Pompey. Your hostages I have, so have you mine;
And we shall talk before we fight.
  Caesar.   Most meet
That first we come to words, and therefore have we
Our written purposes before us sent;   4
Which if thou hast consider'd, let us know
If 'twill tie up thy discontented sword,
And carry back to Sicily much tall youth
That else must perish here.
  Pompey.   To you all three,   8
The senators alone of this great world,
Chief factors for the gods, I do not know
Wherefore my father should revengers want,
Having a son and friends, since Julius Caesar,   12
Who at Philippi the good Brutus ghosted,
There saw you laboring for him. What was't
That mov'd pale Cassius to conspire? And what
Made the all-honor'd, honest Roman, Brutus,   16
With the arm'd rest, courtiers of beauteous freedom,
To drench the capitol, but that they would

120 **way's** way as. SD **Enter Pompey** begins II.6. 2 **meet** proper.
7 **tall** sturdy, courageous. 10 **factors** agents. 13 **ghosted** appeared
as a ghost to. 16 **Made the all-honor'd** F *Made all-honor'd.*

Have one man but a man? And that is it
Hath made me rig my navy, at whose burthen   20
The anger'd ocean foams, with which I meant
To scourge th' ingratitude that despiteful Rome
Cast on my noble father.
  Caesar.   Take your time.
  Antony. Thou canst not fear us, Pompey, with thy
     sails;   24
We'll speak with thee at sea. At land, thou know'st
How much we do o'recount thee.
  Pompey.   At land, indeed,
Thou dost o'recount me of my father's house:
But since the cuckoo builds not for himself,   28
Remain in't as thou mayst.
  Lepidus.   Be pleas'd to tell us—
For this is from the present—how you take
The offers we have sent you.
  Caesar.   There's the point.
  Antony. Which do not be entreated to,   32
But weigh what it is worth embrac'd.
  Caesar. And what may follow to try a larger for-
     tune.
  Pompey. You have made me offer
Of Sicily, Sardinia; and I must   36
Rid all the sea of pirates; then, to send
Measures of wheat to Rome; this 'greed upon,
To part with unhack'd edges, and bear back   39
Our targes undinted.

19 is F *his*. 24 fear frighten. 25 **speak** meet in conflict. 26 o'recount N. 26-9 At land . . . mayst N. 28 **cuckoo** the cuckoo never
builds a nest but lays its eggs in the nests of other birds. 29 **mayst**
canst. 30 **from the present** irrelevant to the present purpose.
33 **embrac'd** if accepted. 34 **to . . . fortune** N. 39 **To part . . .**
edges to depart without battle. 40 **targes** shields.

Omnes.　　　　　That's our offer.

Pompey.　　　　　　　　　Know, then,
I came before you here a man prepar'd
To take this offer; but Mark Antony
Put me to some impatience. Though I lose
The praise of it by telling, you must know,　　44
When Caesar and your brother were at blows,
Your mother came to Sicily and did find
Her welcome friendly.

Antony.　　　　　I have heard it, Pompey,
And am well studied for a liberal thanks　　48
Which I do owe you.

Pompey.　　　　Let me have your hand:
I did not think, sir, to have met you here.

Antony. The beds i' th' east are soft; and thanks
　　to you,
That call'd me timelier than my purpose hither,　52
For I have gain'd by't.

Caesar.　　　　Since I saw you last,
There's a change upon you.

Pompey.　　　　Well, I know not
What counts harsh Fortune casts upon my face,
But in my bosom shall she never come　　56
To make my heart her vassal.

Lepidus.　　　　　Well met here.

Pompey. I hope so, Lepidus. Thus we are agreed:
I crave our composition may be written
And seal'd between us.

Caesar.　　　　That's the next to do.　　60

Pompey. We'll feast each other ere we part, and
　　let's

40 Omnes i.e. Caesar, Antony, Lepidus. 46–7 Your . . . friendly
N. 48 am well . . . thanks I am ready to thank you very much.
52 timelier earlier. 55 counts N. 59 composition agreement.

47

Draw lots who shall begin.

Antony.   That will I, Pompey.

Pompey. No, Antony, take the lot:

But, first or last, your fine Egyptian cookery   64

Shall have the fame. I have heard that Julius Caesar

Grew fat with feasting there.

Antony.   You have heard much.

Pompey. I have fair meanings, sir.

Antony.   And fair words to them.

Pompey. Then, so much have I heard;   68

And I have heard Apollodorus carried—

Enobarbus. No more of that: he did so.

Pompey.   What, I pray you?

Enobarbus. A certain queen to Caesar in a mattress.

Pompey. I know thee now; how far'st thou, soldier?

Enobarbus.   Well;

And well am like to do, for I perceive   73

Four feasts are toward.

Pompey.   Let me shake thy hand;

I never hated thee: I have seen thee fight,

When I have envied thy behavior.   76

Enobarbus. Sir, I never lov'd you much, but I ha'
      prais'd ye

When you have well deserv'd ten times as much

As I have said you did.

Pompey.   Enjoy thy plainness,

It nothing ill becomes thee.   80

Aboard my galley I invite you all:

Will you lead, lords?

All.   Show's the way, sir.

65 Shall . . . fame shall have the opportunity to show that it
deserves its reputation; shall win the prize. 70 more of that F
more that. 74 toward in prospect. 80 nothing not at all. 82 All
i.e. the triumvirs.

Pompey.   Come.

      Exeunt. Mane[n]t Enobarbus and Menas.

Menas. Thy father, Pompey, would ne're have made
this treaty. You and I have known, sir.   84

Enobarbus. At sea, I think.

Menas. We have, sir.

Enobarbus. You have done well by water.

Menas. And you by land.   88

Enobarbus. I will praise any man that will praise
me; though it cannot be denied what I have done by
land.

Menas. Nor what I have done by water.   92

Enobarbus. Yes, something you can deny for your
own safety; you have been a great thief by sea.

Menas. And you by land.   95

Enobarbus. There I deny my land service. But give
me your hand, Menas; if our eyes had authority,
here they might take two thieves kissing.

Menas. All men's faces are true, whatsomere their
hands are.   100

Enobarbus. But there is never a fair woman has a
true face.

Menas. No slander; they steal hearts.

Enobarbus. We came hither to fight with you.   104

Menas. For my part, I am sorry it is turn'd to a
drinking. Pompey doth this day laugh away his fortune.

Enobarbus. If he do, sure he cannot weep't back
again.   109

Menas. Y' have said, sir. We looked not for Mark

---

84 **known** met. 98 **authority** i.e. to arrest criminals. **take** arrest.
98 **two thieves kissing** our hands clasping (with perhaps a glance
at ll. 93–4). 99 **true** honest. **whatsomere** whatsome'er. 110
Y' have said you are perfectly right.

Antony here: pray you, is he married to Cleopatra?

Enobarbus. Caesar's sister is call'd Octavia. 112

Menas. True, sir; she was the wife of Caius Marcellus.

Enobarbus. But she is now the wife of Marcus Antonius. 116

Menas. Pray ye, sir?

Enobarbus. 'Tis true.

Menas. Then is Caesar and he for ever knit together. 120

Enobarbus. If I were bound to divine of this unity, I would not prophesy so.

Menas. I think the policy of that purpose made more in the marriage than the love of the parties.

Enobarbus. I think so too. But you shall find the band that seems to tie their friendship together will be the very strangler of their amity: Octavia is of a holy, cold, and still conversation. 128

Menas. Who would not have his wife so?

Enobarbus. Not he that himself is not so: which is Mark Antony. He will to his Egyptian dish again: then shall the sighs of Octavia blow the fire up in Caesar, and, as I said before, that which is the strength of their amity shall prove the immediate author of their variance. Antony will use his affection where it is. He married but his occasion here.

Menas. And thus it may be. Come, sir, will you aboard? I have a health for you. 138

Enobarbus. I shall take it, sir: we have us'd our throats in Egypt.

117 **Pray ye, sir?** phrase expressing surprise and incredulity. 121 **unity** compact. 123-4 **made more in** had more to do with. 128 **conversation** demeanor, disposition. 135-6 **will use . . . is** will keep loving where he now loves, i.e. in Egypt. 136 **occasion** convenience.

Menas. Come, let's away.   *Exeunt.*

*Music plays. Enter two or three Servants,
with a banket.*

1. [Servant.] Here they'll be, man. Some o' their
plants are ill-rooted already; the least wind i' th'
world will blow them down.

2. [Servant.] Lepidus is high-color'd.   4

1. [Servant.] They have made him drink alms-
drink.

2. [Servant.] As they pinch one another by the
disposition, he cries out, 'No more'; reconciles them
to his entreaty, and himself to th' drink.   9

1. [Servant.] But it raises the greater war between
him and his discretion.   11

2. [Servant.] Why, this it is to have a name in
great men's fellowship. I had as live have a reed that
will do me no service as a partisan I could not heave.

1. [Servant.] To be call'd into a huge sphere and
not to be seen to move in't are the holes where eyes
should be, which pitifully disaster the cheeks.   17

*A sennet sounded. Enter Caesar, Antony, Pompey,
Lepidus, Agrippa, Maecenas, Enobarbus, Menas,
with other Captains.*

Antony. Thus do they, sir: they take the flow o' th'
Nile

SD **Music plays** begins II.7. 1 **o' their** F *o' th' their.* 2 **plants** pun
on two meanings: 'young trees,' and 'soles of the feet.' 5–6 **alms-
drink** toast drunk for one too infirm to answer a pledge. 7–8
As . . . disposition whenever they start a quarrel. 13 **live** lief.
14 **partisan** spear, pike. 15–17 **To be call'd . . . cheeks** N. 17
disaster ruin. SD **sennet** set of notes on trumpet announcing
the approach or entrance of an important person. **Menas** F
Menes.

By certain scales i' th' pyramid; they know   19
By th' height, the lowness, or the mean, if dearth
Or foison follow. The higher Nilus swells
The more it promises: as it ebbs, the seedsman
Upon the slime and ooze scatters his grain,
And shortly comes to harvest.   24

Lepidus. Y' have strange serpents there?

Antony. Ay, Lepidus.

Lepidus. Your serpent of Egypt is bred now of
your mud by the operation of your sun: so is your
crocodile.   29

Antony. They are so.

Pompey. Sit—and some wine! A health to Lepidus!

Lepidus. I am not so well as I should be, but I'll
ne're out.   33

Enobarbus. Not till you have slept; I fear me you'll
be in till then.

Lepidus. Nay, certainly, I have heard the Ptolemies' pyramises are very goodly things; without con-
tradiction I have heard that.   38

Menas. Pompey, a word.

Pompey.   Say in mine ear, what is't?

Menas. Forsake thy seat, I do beseech thee, captain,
                                        Whispers in's ear.

And hear me speak a word.

Pompey.   Forbear me till anon.

This wine for Lepidus!   42

Lepidus. What manner o' thing is your crocodile?

Antony. It is shap'd, sir, like itself, and it is as
broad as it hath breadth; it is just so high as it is,

19 scales graduations. 20 **dearth** scarcity. 21 foison abundance.
32–3 I'll ne're out I'll never give up. 37 pyramises N. **goodly**
handsome. SD **Whisper . . . ear** F prints SD after *anon,* l. 41.
52

and moves with it own organs. It lives by that which
nourisheth it, and the elements once out of it, it
transmigrates.   48
  Lepidus. What color is it of?
  Antony. Of it own color too.
  Lepidus. 'Tis a strange serpent.
  Antony. 'Tis so, and the tears of it are wet.   52
  Caesar. Will this description satisfy him?
  Antony. With the health that Pompey gives him,
else he is a very epicure.   [*Menas whispers again.*]
  Pompey. Go hang, sir, hang! Tell me of that?
    away!   56
Do as I bid you. Where's this cup I call'd for?
  Menas. If for the sake of merit thou wilt hear me,
Rise from thy stool.
  Pompey.   I think th' art mad. The matter?
  Menas. I have ever held my cap off to thy fortunes.
  Pompey. Thou hast serv'd me with much faith.
    What's else to say?   61
Be jolly, lords.
  Antony.   These quicksands, Lepidus,
Keep off them, for you sink.
  Menas. Wilt thou be lord of all the world?
  Pompey.   What sayst thou?
  Menas. Wilt thou be lord of the whole world? That's
    twice.   65
  Pompey. How should that be?
  Menas.   But entertain it,
And though thou think me poor, I am the man
Will give thee all the world.

46 it own its own. 47 elements principle of life. 48 **transmigrates**
dies (with facetious allusion to doctrine of transmigration of
souls). 60 I have . . . fortunes I have ever been your faithful
follower. 66 But entertain it only accept it (the idea).

Pompey.   Hast thou drunk well?

Menas. No, Pompey, I have kept me from the cup.
Thou art, if thou dar'st be, the earthly Jove: 70
Whatere the ocean pales or sky inclips
Is thine, if thou wilt ha't.

Pompey.   Show me which way.

Menas. These three world-sharers, these competitors,
Are in thy vessel. Let me cut the cable,
And when we are put off fall to their throats: 75
All there is thine.

Pompey.   Ah, this thou shouldst have done,
And not have spoke on't. In me 'tis villainy;
In thee't had bin good service. Thou must know
'Tis not my profit that does lead mine honor;
Mine honor it. Repent that ere thy tongue   80
Hath so betray'd thine act. Being done unknown,
I should have found it afterwards well done,
But must condemn it now. Desist, and drink.

Menas. [*Aside.*] For this,   84
I'll never follow thy pall'd fortunes more.
Who seeks and will not take when once 'tis offer'd
Shall never find it more.

Pompey.   This health to Lepidus!

Antony. Bear him ashore. I'll pledge it for him,
    Pompey.   88

Enobarbus. Here's to thee, Menas!

Menas.   Enobarbus, welcome!

Pompey. Fill till the cup be hid.

Enobarbus. There's a strong fellow, Menas.

Menas. Why?   92

---

68 Hast . . . well? Are you drunk? 71 pales encloses. **inclips**
embraces. 73 **competitors** partners. 85 **pall'd** weakened.

Enobarbus. A' bears the third part of the world,
man; see'st not?

Menas. The third part then is drunk; would it were all,
That it might go on wheels!   96

Enobarbus. Drink thou; increase the reels.

Menas. Come.

Pompey. This is not yet an Alexandrian feast.

Antony. It ripens towards it. Strike the vessels, ho!
Here's to Caesar!

Caesar.   I could well forbear't.   101
It's monstrous labor, when I wash my brain
And it grows fouler.

Antony.   Be a child o' th' time.

Caesar. Possess it, I'll make answer: 104
But I had rather fast from all four days
Than drink so much in one.

Enobarbus. Ha! my brave emperor;
Shall we dance now the Egyptian Bacchanals,   108
And celebrate our drink?

Pompey.   Let's ha't, good soldier.

Antony. Come, let's all take hands,
Till that the conquering wine hath steep'd our sense
In soft and delicate Lethe.

Enobarbus.   All take hands.   112
Make battery to our ears with the loud music;
The while I'll place you; then the boy shall sing.
The holding every man shall bear as loud

93 **A'** he. 95 **then is** F *then he is.* 95–6 **would . . . wheels** N. 97
reels revels N. 100 **Strike the vessels** broach the wine casks.
102 **monstrous** abnormal. 104 **Possess it** drink it off. **I'll . . .
answer** I'll drink to your pledge. 107 **brave** magnificent. 112
Lethe forgetfulness. 113 **Make battery to** assault. 115 **The holding**
the burden or refrain of the song. **bear** keep going (the refrain);
F *beate.*

As his strong sides can volley.   116
  Music plays. Enobarbus places them hand in hand.

            The Song
        Come, thou monarch of the vine,
        Plumpy Bacchus, with pink eyne!
        In thy fats our cares be drown'd,
        With thy grapes our hairs be crown'd.
          Cup us, till the world go round,
          Cup us, till the world go round!   122

  Caesar. What would you more? Pompey, good
      night. Good brother,
Let me request you off: our graver business
Frowns at this levity. Gentle lords, let's part;
You see we have burnt our cheeks; strong Enobarb
Is weaker than the wine, and mine own tongue   127
Splits what it speaks; the wild disguise hath almost
Antick'd us all. What needs more words? Good night.
Good Antony, your hand.   130
  Pompey. I'll try you on the shore.
  Antony.   And shall, sir. Give's your hand.
  Pompey. O, Antony, you have my father's house,
But what, we are friends! Come down into the boat.
  Enobarbus. Take heed you fall not. Menas, I'll not
      on shore.   [*Exeunt Pompey, Caesar, Antony,
                              and Attendants.*]
  Menas. No, to my cabin.

---

118 **pink** small, half-closed. **eyne** eyes. 119 **fats** vats. 124 **request
you off** beg you to come away. 126 **we have** read 'we've.' 128
Splits F *Spleet's.* **speaks; the** F *speakest: he.* 129 **Antick'd us**
turned us into grotesque buffoons. 131 **I'll try . . . shore** N.
Give's F *giues.* 132 **father's** F *Father.* 134–8 **Take heed . . .
out** N.

56

These drums! these trumpets, flutes! what!   136
Let Neptune hear we bid a loud farewell
To these great fellows. Sound and be hang'd! Sound
    out!   *Sound a flourish with drums.*
Enobarbus. Hoo! says a. There's my cap.
Menas. Hoa! noble captain! Come.   *Exeunt.*

*Enter Ventidius, as it were in triumph, the dead body
    of Pacorus borne before him.*

Ventidius. Now, darting Parthia, art thou struck;
    and now
Pleas'd fortune does of Marcus Crassus' death
Make me revenger. Bear the king's son's body
Before our army. Thy Pacorus, Orodes,   4
Pays this for Marcus Crassus.
Roman.   Noble Ventidius,
Whilst yet with Parthian blood thy sword is warm,
The fugitive Parthians follow. Spur through Media,
Mesopotamia, and the shelters whither   8
The routed fly: so thy grand captain Antony
Shall set thee on triumphant chariots and
Put garlands on thy head.
Ventidius.   O Silius, Silius,
I have done enough. A lower place, note well,   12
May make too great an act. For learn this, Silius,
Better to leave undone than by our deed
Acquire too high a fame when him we serve's away.
Caesar and Antony have ever won   16
More in their officer than person. Sossius,

137 hear we F *heere a we.* a loud F *aloud.* SD Enter Ventidius
begins III.1. 1 darting Parthia N. struck defeated; F *stroke.*
4–5 Thy Pacorus . . . Crassus N. 4 Orodes F *Orades.* 5 this i.e,
death. Roman N. 12 A lower place a subordinate. 15 serve's F
serues.

57

One of my place in Syria, his lieutenant,
For quick accumulation of renown,
Which he achiev'd by th' minute, lost his favor.   20
Who does i' th' wars more than his captain can
Becomes his captain's captain: and ambition,
The soldier's virtue, rather makes choice of loss
Than gain which darkens him.   24
I could do more to do Antonius good,
But 'twould offend him; and in his offense
Should my performance perish.
   Roman.   Thou hast, Ventidius, that
Without the which a soldier and his sword   28
Grants scarce distinction. Thou wilt write to Antony?
   Ventidius. I'll humbly signify what in his name
That magical word of war, we have effected;
How, with his banners and his well-paid ranks,   32
The ne're-yet-beaten horse of Parthia
We have jaded out o' th' field.
   Roman.   Where is he now?
   Ventidius. He purposeth to Athens, whither, with
     what haste
The weight we must convey with's will permit   36
We shall appear before him. On, there; pass along.
                              Exeunt.

Enter Agrippa at one door, Enobarbus at another.

   Agrippa. What! are the brothers parted?
   Enobarbus. They have dispatch'd with Pompey; he
     is gone;
The other three are sealing. Octavia weeps

20 by th' minute incessantly. 24 darkens obscures (his superior).
26 his offense my offending him. 27–9 Thou hast . . . distinction
N. 34 jaded wearied. SD Enter Agrippa begins III.2. 1 parted
departed. 2 dispatch'd completed their business. 3 sealing signing
and sealing agreements.

To part from Rome; Caesar is sad, and Lepidus,
Since Pompey's feast, as Menas says, is troubl'd   5
With the green-sickness.

Agrippa.   'Tis a noble Lepidus.

Enobarbus. A very fine one. O, how he loves Caesar!

Agrippa. Nay, but how dearly he adores Mark
    Antony!   8

Enobarbus. Caesar? Why, he's the Jupiter of men.

Agrippa. What's Antony? The god of Jupiter.

Enobarbus. Spake you of Caesar? How! the non-
    pareil!

Agrippa. O, Antony! O thou Arabian bird!   12

Enobarbus. Would you praise Caesar, say, 'Caesar':
    go no further.

Agrippa. Indeed, he plied them both with excellent
    praises.

Enobarbus. But he loves Caesar best; yet he loves
    Antony.

Hoo! hearts, tongues, figures, scribes, bards, poets,
    cannot   16

Think, speak, cast, write, sing, number—hoo!—

His love to Antony. But as for Caesar,

Kneel down, kneel down, and wonder.

Agrippa.   Both he loves.

Enobarbus. They are his shards, and he their beetle.
                        [*Trumpets within.*]

This is to horse. Adieu, noble Agrippa.   21

Agrippa. Good fortune, worthy soldier, and fare-
    well.

     Enter Caesar, Antony, Lepidus, and Octavia.

---

6 green-sickness N. 'Tis N. 10 Agrippa F *Ant.* 12 Arabian bird N.
16 figures F *figure.* 17 cast calculate. 20 shards 'wing cases,' here
'wings.'

Antony. No further, sir.

Caesar. You take from me a great part of myself;
Use me well in't. Sister, prove such a wife   25
As my thoughts make thee, and as my farthest band
Shall pass on thy approof. Most noble Antony,
Let not the piece of virtue, which is set   28
Betwixt us as the cyment of our love
To keep it builded, be the ram to batter
The fortress of it: for better might we
Have lov'd without this mean, if on both parts   32
This be not cherish'd.

Antony.   Make me not offended
In your distrust.

Caesar.   I have said.

Antony.   You shall not find,
Though you be therein curious, the least cause   35
For what you seem to fear. So, the gods keep you,
And make the hearts of Romans serve your ends!
We will here part.

Caesar. Farewell, my dearest sister, fare thee well:
The elements be kind to thee, and make   40
Thy spirits all of comfort! fare thee well.

Octavia. My noble brother!

Antony. The April's in her eyes; it is love's spring,
And these the showers to bring it on. Be cheerful.

Octavia. Sir, look well to my husband's house; and—

Caesar.   What, Octavia?

Octavia. I'll tell you in your ear.   46

Antony. Her tongue will not obey her heart, nor can
Her heart obey her tongue; the swan's-down feather

26–7 as my . . . approof N. 27 pass pledge. 29 **cyment** cement
(stressed —′—). 35 **curious** minutely inquiring. 40 **elements** N.
48–50 **the swan's-down . . . inclines** N.

That stands upon the swell at full of tide 49
And neither way inclines.

Enobarbus. [*Aside.*] Will Caesar weep?

Agrippa.   He has a cloud in's face.

Enobarbus. He were the worse for that were he a
   horse; 52
So is he, being a man.

Agrippa.   Why, Enobarbus,
When Antony found Julius Caesar dead,
He cried almost to roaring; and he wept
When at Philippi he found Brutus slain. 56

Enobarbus. That year, indeed, he was troubl'd with
   a rheum;
What willingly he did confound he wail'd.
Believe't, till I wept too.

Caesar.   No, sweet Octavia,
You shall hear from me still; the time shall not 60
Out-go my thinking on you.

Antony.   Come, sir, come;
I'll wrestle with you in my strength of love:
Look, here I have you; thus I let you go,
And give you to the gods.

Caesar.   Adieu; be happy! 64

Lepidus. Let all the number of the stars give light
To thy fair way!

Caesar.   Farewell, farewell! *Kisses Octavia.*

Antony.   Farewell!

                    Trumpets sound. Exeunt.

Enter Cleopatra, Charmian, Iras, and Alexas.

49 at full F *at the full.* 51–2 He has . . . horse N. 57 rheum cold.
58 confound destroy. 59 wept F *Weepe.* 60 still continually.
SD Enter Cleopatra begins III.3.

Cleopatra. Where is the fellow?

Alexas. Half afeard to come.

Cleopatra. Go to, go to. Come hither, sir.

Enter the Messenger as before.

Alexas. Good majesty,
Herod of Jewry dare not look upon you
But when you are well pleas'd.

Cleopatra. That Herod's head
I'll have; but how, when Antony is gone   5
Through whom I might command it? Come thou near.

Messenger. Most gracious majesty!

Cleopatra. Didst thou behold Octavia?

Messenger. Ay, dread queen.

Cleopatra. Where?

Messenger. Madam, in Rome:
I look'd her in the face, and saw her led   9
Between her brother and Mark Antony.

Cleopatra. Is she as tall as me?

Messenger. She is not, madam.

Cleopatra. Didst hear her speak? is she shrill-
    tongu'd or low?   12

Messenger. Madam, I heard her speak; she is low-
    voic'd.

Cleopatra. That's not so good. He cannot like her
    long.

Charmian. Like her! O Isis! 'tis impossible.

Cleopatra. I think so, Charmian: dull of tongue,
    and dwarfish!   16
What majesty is in her gait? Remember,
If ere thou look'st on majesty.

3 **Herod** fierce tyrant of miracle plays. 4–5 **That . . . have** N.
18 **look'st** look'dst N.

Messenger.   She creeps;
Her motion and her station are as one;
She shows a body rather than a life,   20
A statue than a breather.
  Cleopatra.   Is this certain?
  Messenger. Or I have no observance.
  Charmian.   Three in Egypt
Cannot make better note.
  Cleopatra.   He's very knowing,
I do perceive't. There's nothing in her yet.   24
The fellow has good judgment.
  Charmian.   Excellent.
  Cleopatra. Guess at her years, I prithee.
  Messenger. Madam, she was a widow.
  Cleopatra. Widow! Charmian, hark.   28
  Messenger. And I do think she's thirty.
  Cleopatra. Bear'st thou her face in mind? is't long
      or round?
  Messenger. Round even to faultiness.
  Cleopatra. For the most part, too, they are foolish
      that are so.   32
Her hair, what color?
  Messenger. Brown, madam: and her forehead
As low as she would wish it.
  Cleopatra.   There's gold for thee:
Thou must not take my former sharpness ill.   36
I will employ thee back again; I find thee
Most fit for business. Go, make thee ready;
Our letters are prepar'd.   [*Exit Messenger.*]
  Charmian.   A proper man.
  Cleopatra. Indeed, he is so: I repent me much   40

19 **station** manner of standing. 20 **shows** appears to be. 30 **long
or round** N. 34 **Brown** N. 35 **As low . . . it** N. 39 **proper** handsome.

That so I harried him. Why, methinks, by him
This creature's no such thing.

   Charmian.   Nothing, madam.

   Cleopatra. The man hath seen some majesty, and
     should know.   43

   Charmian. Hath he seen majesty? Isis else defend,
And serving you so long!

   Cleopatra. I have one thing more to ask him yet,
     good Charmian:

But 'tis no matter; thou shalt bring him to me
Where I will write. All may be well enough.   48

   Charmian. I warrant you, madam.   *Exeunt.*

Enter Antony and Octavia.

   Antony. Nay, nay, Octavia, not only that,
That were excusable, that and thousands more
Of semblable import, but he hath wag'd
New wars 'gainst Pompey; made his will, and read it
To public ear,   5
Spoke scantly of me; when perforce he could not
But pay me terms of honor, cold and sickly
He vented them; most narrow measure lent me;   8
When the best hint was given him, he not took't,
Or did it from his teeth.

   Octavia.   O my good lord,
Believe not all, or if you must believe,
Stomach not all. A more unhappy lady,   12
If this division chance, ne're stood between,
Praying for both parts:
The good gods will mock me presently,   15

41 harried maltreated. by him according to his report. SD Enter
Antony begins III.4. 3 semblable similar. 4 made . . . read it N.
8 vented uttered. narrow measure lent me gave me little credit.
9 took't F *look't.* 10 from his teeth grudgingly. 15 presently
instantly.

When I shall pray 'O, bless my lord and husband';
Undo that prayer, by crying out as loud,
'O, bless my brother!' Husband win, win brother,
Prays and destroys the prayer; no midway
'Twixt these extremes at all.

Antony.   Gentle Octavia,   20
Let your best love draw to that point which seeks
Best to preserve it. If I lose mine honor
I lose myself: better I were not yours   23
Than yours so branchless. But, as you requested,
Yourself shall go between's; the mean time, lady,
I'll raise the preparation of a war
Shall stain your brother; make your soonest haste,
So your desires are yours.

Octavia.   Thanks to my lord.   28
The Jove of power make me, most weak, most weak,
Your reconciler! Wars 'twixt you twain would be
As if the world shall cleave, and that slain men
Should soader up the rift.   32

Antony. When it appears to you where this begins,
Turn your displeasure that way; for our faults
Can never be so equal that your love   35
Can equally move with them. Provide your going;
Choose your own company, and command what cost
Your heart has mind to.   *Exeunt.*

Enter Enobarbus and Eros.

Enobarbus. How now, friend Eros!
Eros. There's strange news come, sir.
Enobarbus. What, man?

---

24 **branchless** mutilated. 27 **Shall stain** that will stain. 31 **that**
repeats *as if.* 32 **soader** solder. 38 **has** F *he's.* SD **Enter Enobarbus**
begins III.5.

Eros. Caesar and Lepidus have made wars upon
Pompey.   5

Enobarbus. This is old: what is the success?

Eros. Caesar, having made use of him in the wars
'gainst Pompey, presently denied him rivality, would
not let him partake in the glory of the action, and
not resting here, accuses him of letters he had for-
merly wrote to Pompey; upon his own appeal seizes
him: so the poor third is up, till death enlarge his
confine.   13

Enobarbus. Then, world, thou hast a pair of chaps,
no more;
And throw between them all the food thou hast,
They'll grind the one the other. Where's Antony?

Eros. He's walking in the garden—thus, and spurns
The rush that lies before him; cries, 'Fool, Lepidus!'
And threats the throat of that his officer
That murdred Pompey.

Enobarbus.   Our great navy's rigg'd.   20

Eros. For Italy and Caesar. More, Domitius;
My lord desires you presently: my news
I might have told hereafter.

Enobarbus.   'Twill be naught;
But let it be. Bring me to Antony.   24

Eros. Come, sir.   *Exeunt.*

Enter Agrippa, Maecenas, and Caesar.

6 success outcome. **8 presently** immediately. **rivality** partnership.
11 upon his own appeal on his own (Caesar's) accusation. **12 is
up** imprisoned. **enlarge his confine** set him free. **14 Then, world,
thou hast** F *Then would thou hadst.* **chaps** jaws. **16 the one the
other** F *the other.* **19 that his officer** that officer of his N. **20 navy's**
F *Nauies.* SD **Enter Agrippa** begins III.6.

Caesar. Contemning Rome, he has done all this and
    more
In Alexandria; here's the manner of't:
I' th' market place, on a tribunal silver'd,
Cleopatra and himself in chairs of gold   4
Were publicly enthron'd: at the feet sat
Caesarion, whom they call my father's son,
And all the unlawful issue that their lust
Since then hath made between them. Unto her   8
He gave the stablishment of Egypt; made her
Of Lower Syria, Cyprus, Lydia, absolute queen.
    Maecenas. This in the public eye?
    Caesar. I' th' common show place, where they exer-
    cise.   12
His sons he there proclaim'd the kings of kings;
Great Media, Parthia, and Armenia
He gave to Alexander; to Ptolemy he assign'd
Syria, Cilicia, and Phoenicia. She   16
In th' habiliments of the goddess Isis
That day appear'd, and oft before gave audience,
As 'tis reported, so.
    Maecenas. Let Rome be thus inform'd.   20
    Agrippa. Who, queasy with his insolence already,
Will their good thoughts call from him.
    Caesar. The people knows it,
And have now receiv'd his accusations.   24
    Agrippa. Who does he accuse?
    Caesar. Caesar, and that, having in Sicily
Sextus Pompeius spoil'd, we had not rated him   27

---

1 Contemning scorning. he has read 'he's.' **3 tribunal** raised plat-
form. **6 my father's son** N. **9 stablishment** government, rule.
10 Lydia N. **12–19 I' th' common . . . so** N. **13 he there** F
hither. **the kings** F *the King*. **17 Isis** See I.2.69 N above. **21
queasy** nauseated. **27 spoil'd** despoiled of his territories. **rated
him** assigned to him.

His part o' th' isle; then does he say, he lent me
Some shipping unrestor'd; lastly, he frets
That Lepidus of the triumvirate should be depos'd;
And, being, that we detain all his revenue.

Agrippa. Sir, this should be answer'd.   32

Caesar. 'Tis done already, and the messenger gone.
I have told him Lepidus was grown too cruel;
That he his high authority abus'd,
And did deserve his change: for what I have con-
    quer'd,   36
I grant him part: but then, in his Armenia,
And other of his conquer'd kingdoms, I
Demand the like.

Maecenas.   He'll never yield to that.   39

Caesar. Nor must not then be yielded to in this.

Enter Octavia, with her train.

Octavia. Hail, Caesar, and my lord; hail, most dear
    Caesar!

Caesar. That ever I should call thee castaway!

Octavia. You have not call'd me so, nor have you
    cause.

Caesar. Why have you stol'n upon us thus? You
    come not   44
Like Caesar's sister; the wife of Antony
Should have an army for an usher, and
The neighs of horse to tell of her approach
Long ere she did appear; the trees by th' way   48
Should have borne men, and expectation fainted,
Longing for what it had not; nay, the dust
Should have ascended to the roof of heaven,
Rais'd by your populous troops. But you are come

30 triumvirate F *Triumpherate.* 31 revenue stressed — —' —.
36 I have read 'I've.' 47 horse horses.

A market-maid to Rome, and have prevented   53
The ostentation of our love, which, left unshown,
Is often left unlov'd: we should have met you
By sea and land, supplying every stage   56
With an augmented greeting.

Octavia.   Good my lord,
To come thus was I not constrain'd, but did it
On my free will. My lord, Mark Antony,   59
Hearing that you prepar'd for war, acquainted
My grieved ear withal: whereon, I begg'd
His pardon for return.

Caesar.   Which soon he granted,   62
Being an abstract 'tween his lust and him.

Octavia. Do not say so, my lord.

Caesar.   I have eyes upon him,
And his affairs come to me on the wind.
Where is he now?

Octavia.   My lord, in Athens.   66

Caesar. No, my most wronged sister; Cleopatra
Hath nodded him to her. He hath given his empire
Up to a whore, who now are levying   69
The kings o' th' earth for war. He hath assembl'd
Bocchus the King of Libya, Archelaus
Of Cappadocia, Philadelphos, King   72
Of Paphlagonia, the Thracian king, Adallas,
King Manchus of Arabia, King of Pont,
Herod of Jewry, Mithridates, King
Of Comageat, Polemon and Amintas,   76

54–5 The ostentation . . . unlov'd N. 61 withal with it. 62 **pardon**
permission. 63 **Being an abstract . . . him** N. 68 **He hath given**
read 'He'th giv'n.' 69 **who** i.e. Antony and Cleopatra. 71 **Libya**
North Africa exclusive of Egypt. 72 **Cappadocia** Roman province
in East Asia Minor. 73 **Paphlagonia** Roman province in North
Asia Minor. **Adallas** F *Adullas*. 74 **Manchus** F *Mauchus*. **Pont**
Pontus. 76 **Comageat** Comagene.

The Kings of Mede and Lycaonia;
With a more larger list of scepters.
  Octavia. Ay me, most wretched,
That have my heart parted betwixt two friends   80
That do afflict each other!
  Caesar.   Welcome hither:
Your letters did withhold our breaking forth,
Till we perceiv'd both how you were wrong led
And we in negligent danger. Cheer your heart;   84
Be you not troubl'd with the time, which drives
O're your content these strong necessities,
But let determin'd things to destiny
Hold unbewail'd their way. Welcome to Rome,   88
Nothing more dear to me. You are abus'd
Beyond the mark of thought, and the high gods,
To do you justice, makes his ministers   91
Of us and those that love you. Best of comfort,
And ever welcome to us.
  Agrippa.   Welcome, lady.
  Maecenas. Welcome, dear madam.
Each heart in Rome does love and pity you;
Only th' adulterous Antony, most large   96
In his abominations, turns you off,
And gives his potent regiment to a trull,
That noises it against us.
  Octavia.   Is it so, sir?   99
  Caesar. Most certain. Sister, welcome; pray you,

---

77 **Mede** Media. **Lycaonia** Roman province in South Asia Minor;
F *Licoania*. 81 do F *does*. **afflict** clash with. 83 **wrong led** N. 84
negligent danger danger which we neglected. 90 **mark** range
(metaphor from archery). 91 **makes his** N. 96 **large** unrestrained.
98 **potent regiment** powerful rule. **trull** harlot. 99 **noises it** is
clamorous.

Be ever know to patience. My dear'st sister! *Exeunt.*

Enter Cleopatra and Enobarbus.

Cleopatra. I will be even with thee, doubt it not.
Enobarbus. But why, why, why?
Cleopatra. Thou hast forspoke my being in these wars,
And sayst it is not fit.
Enobarbus.   Well, is it, is it? 4
Cleopatra. Is't not denounc'd against us? Why should not we
Be there in person?
Enobarbus. [*Aside.*]   Well, I could reply:
If we should serve with horse and mares together,
The horse were merely lost; the mares would bear
A soldier and his horse.
Cleopatra.   What is't you say? 9
Enobarbus. Your presence needs must puzzle Antony;
Take from his heart, take from his brain, from's time,
What should not then be spar'd. He is already 12
Traduc'd for levity, and 'tis said in Rome
That Photinus an eunuch and your maids
Manage this war.
Cleopatra.   Sink Rome, and their tongues rot
That speak against us! A charge we bear i' th' war,
And as the president of my kingdom will 17
Appear there for a man. Speak not against it;
I will not stay behind.

101 Be . . . patience remain calm at all times. SD Enter Cleopatra begins III.7. 3 forspoke spoken against. 4 it is F *it it.* 5 Is't not denounc'd F *If not, denounc'd* N. denounc'd proclaimed, declared. 8 merely utterly. 10 puzzle paralyze. 13–15 'tis said . . . war N. 16 charge responsibility.

Enter Antony and Canidius.

Enobarbus.   Nay, I have done.   19
Here comes the emperor.
    Antony.   Is it not strange, Canidius,
That from Tarentum and Brundusium
He could so quickly cut the Ionian sea,
And take in Toryne? You have heard on't, sweet?
    Cleopatra. Celerity is never more admir'd   24
Than by the negligent.
    Antony.   A good rebuke,
Which might have well becom'd the best of men
To taunt at slackness. Canidius, we
Will fight with him by sea.
    Cleopatra.   By sea! What else?   28
    Canidius. Why will my lord do so?
    Antony.   For that he dares us to't.
    Enobarbus. So hath my lord dar'd him to single
fight.
    Canidius. Ay, and to wage this battle at Pharsalia,
Where Caesar fought with Pompey. But these offers,
Which serve not for his vantage, he shakes off;   33
And so should you.
    Enobarbus.   Your ships are not well mann'd;
Your mariners are muleters, reapers, people
Ingross'd by swift impress; in Caesar's fleet   36
Are those that often have 'gainst Pompey fought:
Their ships are yare, yours, heavy: no disgrace
Shall fall you for refusing him at sea,
Being prepar'd for land.

21 **Tarentum** Taranto. **Brundusium** Brindisi. 23 **take in** capture.
Toryne F *Troine;* l. 55, *Toryne.* **on't** of it. 29 **For that** because.
35 **muleters** mule-drivers; F *Militers.* 36 **Ingross'd** gathered.
impress conscription. 38 **yare** light, easy to handle. 39 **fall** befall.

Antony. By sea, by sea. 40
Enobarbus. Most worthy sir, you therein throw
  away
The absolute soldiership you have by land,
Distract your army, which doth most consist
Of war-mark'd footmen, leave unexecuted 44
Your own renowned knowledge, quite forgo
The way which promises assurance, and
Give up yourself merely to chance and hazard
From firm security.
  Antony. I'll fight at sea. 48
  Cleopatra. I have sixty sails, Caesar none better.
  Antony. Our overplus of shipping will we burn;
And with the rest full-mann'd, from th' head of
  Actium
Beat th' approaching Caesar. But if we fail, 52
We then can do't at land.

Enter a Messenger.

Thy business?
  Messenger. The news is true, my lord, he is de-
  scried;
Caesar has taken Toryne. 55
  Antony. Can he be there in person? 'tis impossible;
Strange that his power should be. Canidius,
Our nineteen legions thou shalt hold by land,
And our twelve thousand horse. We'll to our ship:
Away, my Thetis!

Enter a Soldier.

How now, worthy soldier? 60

42 **absolute soldiership** perfect generalship. 43 **Distract** divide.
51 **head** headland. **Actium** on the coast of Epirus. 54 **descried**
seen. 57 **power** forces. 60 **Thetis** sea goddess.

Soldier. O noble emperor, do not fight by sea;
Trust not to rotten planks: do you misdoubt
This sword and these my wounds? Let th' Egyptians
And the Phoenicians go a-ducking; we   64
Have us'd to conquer standing on the earth
And fighting foot to foot.

Antony.   Well, well: away!
          Ex[eunt] Antony, Cleopatra, and Enobarbus.
Soldier. By Hercules, I think I am i' th' right.
Canidius. Soldier, thou art: but his whole action
          grows   68
Not in the power on't: so our leader's led,
And we are women's men.

Soldier.   You keep by land
The legions and the horse whole, do you not?

Canidius. Marcus Octavius, Marcus Justeius,   72
Publicola, and Caelius are for sea;
But we keep whole by land. This speed of Caesar's
Carries beyond belief.

Soldier.   While he was yet in Rome
His power went out in such distractions   76
As beguil'd all spies.

Canidius.   Who's his lieutenant, hear you?
Soldier. They say, one Taurus.

Canidius.   Well I know the man.

                    Enter a Messenger.

Messenger. The emperor calls Canidius.
Canidius. With news the time's with labor,   80

61–6 O noble emperor . . . foot N. 63 th' Egyptians read 'the
Egyptians.' 68–9 his whole action . . . on't N. 69 leader's led F
Leaders leade. 70 men servants. 72 **Canidius** F *Ven.* 75 **Carries**
makes headway. 76 **distractions** detachments. 78 **Taurus** F
Towrus. 80 time's F *times.*
          74

And throws forth each minute some.   *Exeunt.*

*Enter Caesar [and Taurus] with his army,
marching.*

Caesar. Taurus!
Taurus. My lord?
Caesar. Strike not by land,
Keep whole, provoke not battle   4
Till we have done at sea. Do not exceed
The prescript of this scroll: our fortune lies
Upon this jump.   [*Exeunt.*]

Enter Antony and Enobarbus.

Antony. Set we our squadrons on yond side o' th'
     hill,   8
In eye of Caesar's battle; from which place
We may the number of the ships behold
And so proceed accordingly.   [*Exeunt.*]

*Canidius marcheth with his land army one way over
the stage, and Taurus, the lieutenant of Caesar, the
other way. After their going in is heard the noise of
a sea fight.*

Alarum. Enter Enobarbus.

Enobarbus. Naught, naught, all naught! I can be-
     hold no longer.   12
Th' Antoniad, the Egyptian admiral,
With all their sixty, fly and turn the rudder:
To see't mine eyes are blasted.

81 throws forth N. SD Enter Caesar begins III.8. 5 exceed depart
from. 6 prescript orders. 7 jump hazard. 9 battle troops in battle
array. 10 may can. 12 Naught ruined, lost. 13 admiral flagship.

Enter Scarus.

Scarus. Gods and goddesses, all the whole synod of
them! 16

Enobarbus. What's thy passion?

Scarus. The greater cantle of the world is lost
With very ignorance; we have kiss'd away 19
Kingdoms and provinces.

   Enobarbus.   How appears the fight?

Scarus. On our side like the token'd pestilence,
Where death is sure. Yon ribald-rid nag of Egypt
(Whom leprosy o'ertake), i' th' midst o' th' fight,
When vantage like a pair of twins appear'd, 24
Both as the same, or rather ours the elder,
The breese upon her, like a cow in June,
Hoists sails and flies.

   Enobarbus.   That I beheld: 27
Mine eyes did sicken at the sight, and could not
Endure a further view.

   Scarus.   She once being loof'd,
The noble ruin of her magic, Antony,
Claps on his sea-wing, and (like a doting mallard)
Leaving the fight in heighth, flies after her: 32
I never saw an action of such shame;
Experience, manhood, honor, ne're before
Did violate so itself.

   Enobarbus.   Alack, alack! 35

Enter Canidius.

Canidius. Our fortune on the sea is out of breath,

17 passion cause of your troubled mind. 18 cantle portion. 19 With
by, through. very absolute. we have read 'we've.' 21 like the
token'd pestilence N. 22 ribald-rid licentious; F *ribaudred*. 26
breese gadfly. 29 being loof'd N. 31 mallard drake, eager to follow
his mate.

And sinks most lamentably. Had our general
Been what he knew himself, it had gone well:
O, he has given example for our flight
Most grossly by his own.   40
    Enobarbus. Ay, are your thereabouts? Why, then,
        good night, indeed.
    Canidius. Toward Peloponnesus are they fled.
    Scarus. 'Tis easy to't.
And there I will attend what further comes.   44
    Canidius. To Caesar will I render
My legions and my horse; six kings already
Show me the way of yielding.
    Enobarbus.   I'll yet follow   47
The wounded chance of Antony, though my reason
Sits in the wind against me.   [*Exeunt.*]

Enter Antony with Attendants.

    Antony. Hark! the land bids me tread no more
        upon't;
It is asham'd to bear me. Friends, come hither:
I am so lated in the world that I
Have lost my way for ever. I have a ship   4
Laden with gold, take that, divide it: fly,
And make your peace with Caesar.
    Omnes.   Fly? not we.
    Antony. I have fled myself, and have instructed
        cowards   7
To run and show their shoulders. Friends, be gone;
I have myself resolv'd upon a course

38 **Been . . . himself** been true to himself as shown in the past.
39 **he has** F 'his ha's' N. 43 **to't** F *toot.* 45 **render** surrender. 48
chance fortunes. SD **Enter Antony** begins III.9. 3 **lated** belated.
6 **Omnes** i.e. attendants. 8 **show their shoulders** show their backs.

Which has no need of you. Be gone.
My treasure's in the harbor. Take it. O,
I follow'd that I blush to look upon: 12
My very hairs do mutiny, for the white
Reprove the brown for rashness, and they them
For fear and doting. Friends, be gone; you shall
Have letters from me to some friends that will   16
Sweep your way for you. Pray you, look not sad,
Nor make replies of loathness; take the hint
Which my despair proclaims; let that be left
Which leaves itself; to the seaside straightway;   20
I will possess you of that ship and treasure.
Leave me, I pray, a little: pray you now,
Nay, do so; for, indeed, I have lost command,
Therefore I pray you. I'll see you by and by.   24
                        Sits down.

Enter Cleopatra, led by Charmian, [Iras,] and Eros.

  Eros. Nay, gentle madam, to him, comfort him.
  Iras. Do, most dear queen.
  Charmian. Do! Why, what else?
  Cleopatra. Let me sit down. O Juno!   28
  Antony. No, no, no, no, no.
  Eros. See you here, sir?
  Antony. O fie, fie, fie!
  Charmian. Madam!   32
  Iras. Madam, O good empress!
  Eros. Sir, sir!
  Antony. Yes, my lord, yes. He at Philippi kept
His sword e'ne like a dancer, while I struck   36

12 that what. 17 Sweep your way make easy your reconcilement
to Caesar. 18 hint occasion. 19 that F *them.* 23–4 I have lost . . .
you N. 36 His sword . . . dancer N. struck F *strooke.*
  78

The lean and wrinkled Cassius; and 'twas I
That the mad Brutus ended: he alone
Dealt on lieutenantry, and no practice had   39
In the brave squares of war: yet now—No matter.
  Cleopatra. Ah, stand by.
  Eros. The queen, my lord, the queen.
  Iras. Go to him, madam, speak to him;
He's unqualitied with very shame.   44
  Cleopatra. Well then, sustain me: O!
  Eros. Most noble sir, arise, the queen approaches:
Her head's declin'd, and death will seize her, but
Your comfort makes the rescue.   48
  Antony. I have offended reputation,
A most unnoble swerving.
  Eros.   Sir, the queen.
  Antony. O, whither hast thou led me, Egypt? See,
How I convey my shame out of thine eyes   52
By looking back what I have left behind
Stroy'd in dishonor.
  Cleopatra.   O my lord, my lord.
Forgive my fearful sails: I little thought   55
You would have follow'd.
  Antony.   Egypt, thou knew'st too well
My heart was to thy rudder tied by th' strings,
And thou shouldst tow me after. O're my spirit
The full supremacy thou knew'st, and that
Thy beck might from the bidding of the gods   60
Command me.
  Cleopatra. O, my pardon!
  Antony.   Now I must
To the young man send humble treaties, dodge

37 lean . . . Cassius N. 39 Dealt on lieutenantry fought by
proxy. 40 squares squadrons. 44 unqualitied unmanned. 47 seize
F *cease.* but unless. 52–4 How . . . dishonor N. 58 tow F *stowe.*

And palter in the shifts of lowness, who   63
With half the bulk o' th' world play'd as I pleas'd,
Making and marring fortunes. You did know
How much you were my conqueror, and that
My sword, made weak by my affection, would
Obey it on all cause.

Cleopatra.   Pardon, pardon!   68

Antony. Fall not a tear, I say; one of them rates
All that is won and lost. Give me a kiss;
Even this repays me.
We sent our schoolmaster; is a come back?   72
Love, I am full of lead. Some wine
Within there, and our viands! Fortune knows
We scorn her most when most she offers blows.

                                     Exeunt.

Enter Caesar, Agrippa, Dolabella, [Thidias,]
with others.

Caesar. Let him appear that's come from Antony.
Know you him?

Dolabella.   Caesar, 'tis his schoolmaster:
An argument that he is pluck'd, when hither
He sends so poor a pinion of his wing   4
Which had superfluous kings for messengers
Not many moons gone by.

Enter Ambassador from Antony.

Caesar.   Approach and speak.

Ambassador. Such as I am, I come from Antony:

---

63 **palter** shuffle, play tricks. **the shifts of lowness** tricks of a man
humbled by fortune. 69 **Fall** let fall. **rates** is worth. 72 **schoolmaster** N. **a** he. SD **Enter Caesar** begins III.10. **Thidias** N. 3
argument proof. SD **Enter Ambassador** N.
    80

I was of late as petty to his ends   8
As is the morn dew on the myrtle leaf
To his grand sea.
  Caesar.   Be't so. Declare thine office.
  Ambassador. Lord of his fortunes he salutes thee, and
Requires to live in Egypt; which not granted,   12
He lessens his requests, and to thee sues
To let him breathe between the heavens and earth,
A private man in Athens: this for him.
Next, Cleopatra does confess thy greatness,   16
Submits her to thy might, and of thee craves
The circle of the Ptolemies for her heirs,
Now hazarded to thy grace.
  Caesar.   For Antony,
I have no ears to his request. The queen   20
Of audience nor desire shall fail, so she
From Egypt drive her all-disgraced friend,
Or take his life there: this if she perform,
She shall not sue unheard. So to them both.   24
  Ambassador. Fortune pursue thee!
  Caesar.   Bring him through the bands.
                         [Exit Ambassador.]
[To Thidias.] To try thy eloquence, now 'tis time;
    dispatch.
From Antony win Cleopatra; promise,
And in our name, what she requires; add more,   28
From thine invention, offers. Women are not
In their best fortunes strong, but want will perjure
The ne're-touch'd vestal. Try thy cunning, Thidias;
Make thine own edict for thy pains, which we   32

8–10 as petty . . . sea N. 18 circle crown. 19 Now . . . grace
now lost unless you show favor or mercy. 21 so provided. 22
friend lover. 25 bands troops.

Will answer as a law.
 Thidias.   Caesar, I go.
 Caesar. Observe how Antony becomes his flaw,
And what thou think'st his very action speaks
In every power that moves.
 Thidias.   Caesar, I shall. 36
              Exeunt.

Enter Cleopatra, Enobarbus, Charmian, and Iras.

 Cleopatra. What shall we do, Enobarbus?
 Enobarbus.   Think, and die.
 Cleopatra. Is Antony or we in fault for this?
 Enobarbus. Antony only, that would make his will
Lord of his reason. What though you fled 4
From that great face of war, whose several ranges
Frighted each other? Why should he follow?
The itch of his affection should not then
Have nick'd his captainship, at such a point, 8
When half to half the world oppos'd, he being
The mered question. 'Twas a shame no less
Than was his loss, to course your flying flags,
And leave his navy gazing.
 Cleopatra.   Prithee, peace. 12

Enter the Ambassador, with Antony.

 Antony. Is that his answer?
 Ambassador. Ay, my lord.
 Antony. The queen shall then have courtesy,
So she will yield us up.

34 becomes his flaw behaves in his disgrace. **35–6 what thou . . .
moves** N. **SD Enter Cleopatra** begins III.11. **3 will** desire. **5
ranges** lines of battle. **7 affection** passion. **8 nick'd** made a fool of
N. **10 mered question** definite cause. **11 course** chase. **SD Enter
the** Ambassador see III.9.72 N.

Ambassador.   He says so.   18
Antony. Let her know't.
To the boy Caesar send this grizzled head,
And he will fill thy wishes to the brim
With principalities.
Cleopatra.   That head, my lord?   20
Antony. To him again. Tell him he wears the rose
Of youth upon him, from which the world should note
Something particular: his coin, ships, legions,
May be a coward's, whose ministers would prevail
Under the service of a child as soon   25
As i' th' command of Caesar. I dare him therefore
To lay his gay caparisons apart,
And answer me declin'd, sword against sword,   28
Ourselves alone. I'll write it: follow me.
          [*Exeunt Antony and Ambassador.*]
Enobarbus. Yes, like enough, high-battl'd Caesar will
Unstate his happiness, and be stag'd to th' show
Against a sworder! I see men's judgments are   32
A parcel of their fortunes, and things outward
Do draw the inward quality after them
To suffer all alike. That he should dream,
Knowing all measures, the full Caesar will   36
Answer his emptiness! Caesar, thou hast subdu'd
His judgment too.

Enter a Servant.

23 **Something particular** some personal exploit. 24 **ministers**
agents. 27 **caparisons** equipment. 28 **declin'd** in my fallen fortunes. 30 **high-battl'd** possessed of a victorious army. 31 **Unstate**
strip of state and importance. **be stag'd to th' show** be shown on
the stage in public view. 32 **sworder** gladiator. 33 **parcel** part.
35 **To suffer all alike** so that all deteriorate at the same rate.
36 **all measures** both good and bad fortune.

Servant.   A messenger from Caesar.

Cleopatra. What! no more ceremony? See! my
women   39
Against the blown rose may they stop their nose
That kneel'd unto the buds. Admit him, sir.

                                        [*Exit Servant.*]

Enobarbus. Mine honesty and I begin to square.
The loyalty well held to fools does make
Our faith mere folly: yet he that can endure   44
To follow with allegiance a fall'n lord,
Does conquer him that did his master conquer,
And earns a place i' th' story.

Enter Thidias.

Cleopatra.   Caesar's will?   47

Thidias. Hear it apart.

Cleopatra.   None but friends: say boldly.

Thidias. So, haply, are they friends to Antony.

Enobarbus. He needs as many, sir, as Caesar has,
Or needs not us. If Caesar please, our master
Will leap to be his friend: for us, you know   52
Whose he is we are, and that is Caesar's.

Thidias.   So.
Thus then, thou most renown'd, Caesar entreats
Not to consider in what case thou stand'st
Further than he is Caesar.

Cleopatra.   Go on: right royal.   56

Thidias. He knows that you embrace not Antony
As you did love, but as you fear'd him.

Cleopatra.   O!

Thidias. The scars upon your honor therefore he
Does pity, as constrained blemishes,   60

SD Thidias see III.10.1 N. 49 **haply** very likely. 52 **for as** for.
56 **Caesar** F *caesars.*

Not as deserv'd.

Cleopatra.   He is a god, and knows
What is most right. Mine honor was not yielded,
But conquer'd merely.

Enobarbus.   To be sure of that,
I will ask Antony. Sir, sir, thou art so leaky,   64
That we must leave thee to thy sinking, for
Thy dearest quit thee.   *Exit Enobarbus.*

Thidias.   Shall I say to Caesar
What you require of him? for he partly begs
To be desir'd to give. It much would please him   68
That of his fortunes you should make a staff
To lean upon. But it would warm his spirits
To hear from me you had left Antony,
And put yourself under his shroud,   72
The universal landlord.

Cleopatra.   What's your name?

Thidias. My name is Thidias.

Cleopatra.   Most kind messenger,
Say to great Caesar this: in deputation   75
I kiss his conqu'ring hand; tell him I am prompt
To lay my crown at's feet, and there to kneel.
Tell him from his all-obeying breath I hear
The doom of Egypt.

Thidias.   'Tis your noblest course.
Wisdom and fortune combating together,   80
If that the former dare but what it can,
No chance may shake it. Give me grace to lay
My duty on your hand.

Cleopatra.   Your Caesar's father oft,

---

67 require request. 72 shroud protection. 78 from his read
'from's.' all-obeying which all obey.

When he hath mus'd of taking kingdoms in,   84
Bestow'd his lips on that unworthy place,
As it rain'd kisses.

Enter Antony and Enobarbus.

Antony.   Favors? By Jove that thunders!
What art thou, fellow?
    Thidias.   One that but performs
The bidding of the fullest man and worthiest   88
To have command obey'd.
    Enobarbus.   You will be whipp'd.
    Antony. Approach there! Ah, you kite! Now, gods
    and divels!
Authority melts from me. Of late, when I cried 'Ho!'
Like boys unto a muss, kings would start forth,
And cry, 'Your will?' Have you no ears? I am   93
Antony yet. Take hence this Jack and whip him.

Enter a Servant.

    Enobarbus. 'Tis better playing with a lion's whelp
Than with an old one dying.
    Antony.   Moon and stars!   96
Whip him. Were't twenty of the greatest tributaries
That do acknowledge Caesar, should I find them
So saucy with the hand of—she here, what's her
    name,
Since she was Cleopatra? Whip him, fellows,   100
Till, like a boy, you see him cringe his face
And whine aloud for mercy. Take him hence.
    Thidias. Mark Antony—
    Antony.   Tug him away: being whipp'd,

84 taking . . . in conquering. 86 As as if. 90 divels devils. 91 me.
Of late, when F *me of late. When.* 92 muss scramble. 94 Jack
impudent fellow. 101 cringe distort.

Bring him again. This Jack of Caesar's shall   104
Bear us an arrant to him.
          Exeunt [Attendants] with Thidias.
You were half blasted ere I knew you: ha?
Have I my pillow left unpress'd in Rome,
Forborne the getting of a lawful race,   108
And by a gem of women, to be abus'd
By one that looks on feeders?
  Cleopatra.   Good my lord—
  Antony. You have been a boggler ever:
But when we in our viciousness grow hard—   112
O misery on't!—the wise gods seel our eyes,
In our own filth drop our clear judgments, make us
Adore our errors, laugh at's while we strut
To our confusion.
  Cleopatra.   O! is't come to this?   116
  Antony. I found you as a morsel, cold upon
Dead Caesar's trencher; nay, you were a fragment
Of Cneius Pompey's; besides what hotter hours,
Unregist'red in vulgar fame, you have   120
Luxuriously pick'd out; for I am sure
Though you can guess what temperance should be,
You know not what it is.
  Cleopatra.   Wherefore is this?
  Antony. To let a fellow that will take rewards   124
And say 'God quit you!' be familiar with
My playfellow, your hand, this kingly seal
And plighter of high hearts. O, that I were

104 This F *The.* 105 **arrant** errand. 108 **getting** begetting. 109
abus'd tricked. 110 **feeders** servants. 111 **boggler** fickle creature.
113 **seel** sew up N. 115 **at's** at us. 116 **confusion** destruction.
118 **trencher** wooden platter. 120 **vulgar fame** common report.
121 **Luxuriously** lasciviously. 125 **quit** requite. 127 **plighter**
pledger. 127–9 O, that . . . herd N.

Upon the hill of Basan to outroar   128
The horned herd! for I have savage cause,
And to proclaim it civilly were like
A halter'd neck which does the hangman thank
For being yare about him.

Enter a Servant with Thidias.

                                   Is he whipp'd?   132
  Servant. Soundly, my lord.
  Antony.   Cried he? and begg'd a pardon?
  Servant. He did ask favor.
  Antony. If that thy father live, let him repent   135
Thou wast not made his daughter; and be thou sorry
To follow Caesar in his triumph, since
Thou hast bin whipp'd for following him: henceforth,
The white hand of a lady fever thee,   139
Shake thou to look on't. Get thee back to Caesar,
Tell him thy entertainment: look thou say
He makes me angry with him. For he seems
Proud and disdainful, harping on what I am,
Not what he knew I was. He makes me angry,   144
And at this time most easy 'tis to do't,
When my good stars, that were my former guides,
Have empty left their orbs and shot their fires
Into th' abysm of hell. If he mislike   148
My speech and what is done, tell him he has
Hipparchus, my enfranched bondman, whom
He may at pleasure whip, or hang, or torture,
As he shall like, to quit me. Urge it thou: 152

129 **savage cause** cause enough to go mad. 132 **yare** quick. 133 **a** he. 139 **fever thee** may it (the lady's white hand) throw you into a fever. 141 **thy entertainment** your reception (here). 147 **orbs** spheres N. 150 **Hipparchus** N. **enfranched** freed. 152 **quit** pay back. **Urge** mention.

Hence with thy stripes, be gone!   *Exit Thidias.*
   Cleopatra.   Have you done yet?
   Antony. Alack! our terrene moon is now eclips'd,
And it portends alone the fall of Antony.
   Cleopatra. I must stay his time.   156
   Antony. To flatter Caesar, would you mingle eyes
With one that ties his points?
   Cleopatra.   Not know me yet?
   Antony. Cold-hearted toward me?
   Cleopatra.   Ah! dear, if I be so,
From my cold heart let heaven engender hail,   160
And poison it in the source, and the first stone
Drop in my neck: as it determines, so
Dissolve my life. The next Caesarion smite
Till by degrees the memory of my womb,   164
Together with my brave Egyptians all,
By the discandying of this pelleted storm,
Lie graveless, till the flies and gnats of Nile
Have buried them for prey!
   Antony.   I am satisfied.   168
Caesar sets down in Alexandria, where
I will oppose his fate. Our force by land
Hath nobly held; our sever'd navy too
Have knit again, and fleet, threat'ning most sealike.
Where hast thou been, my heart? Dost thou hear,
     lady?   173
If from the field I shall return once more
To kiss these lips, I will appear in blood;
I and my sword will earn our chronicle: 176

154 **our terrene . . . eclips'd** N. 158 **one . . . points** his valet.
162 **determines** melts. 165 **brave** noble. 166 **discandying** dissolving; F *discandering.* 169 **sets** sits. 172 **fleet** are afloat. 175 **in blood** both 'covered with blood' and 'in full vigor' (said of a stag). 176 **earn our chronicle** earn a place in history.

There's hope in't yet.

Cleopatra. That's my brave lord!

Antony. I will be treble-sinew'd, hearted, breath'd,
And fight maliciously: for when mine hours
Were nice and lucky, men did ransom lives   180
Of me for jests; but now I'll set my teeth,
And send to darkness all that stop me. Come,
Let's have one other gaudy night: call to me
All my sad captains; fill our bowls once more: 184
Let's mock the midnight bell.

Cleopatra. It is my birth-day:
I had thought t' have held it poor. But, since my lord
Is Antony again, I will be Cleopatra.

Antony. We will yet do well.   188

Cleopatra. Call all his noble captains to my lord.

Antony. Do so, we'll speak to them; and tonight I'll
    force
The wine peep through their scars. Come on, my
    queen;
There's sap in't yet. The next time I do fight   192
I'll make death love me, for I will contend
Even with his pestilent scythe.

Exeunt [all but Enobarbus].

Enobarbus. Now he'll outstare the lightning. To be
    furious
Is to be frighted out of fear, and in that mood   196
The dove will peck the estridge; and I see still,
A diminution in our captain's brain
Restores his heart. When valor preys on reason
It eats the sword it fights with. I will seek   200

179 **maliciously** fiercely. 180 **nice** in a light mood (wanton?).
183 **gaudy** festive, with joyous revel. 192 **There's . . . yet** there
is life in it still. 194 **Even** read 'e'en.' 197 **estridge** N. 199 **preys on**
F *prays in.*

Some way to leave him.   *Exit.*

Enter Caesar, Agrippa, and Maecenas, with
his army, Caesar reading a letter.

Caesar. He calls me boy, and chides as he had
     power
To beat me out of Egypt. My messenger
He hath whipp'd with rods, dares me to personal
     combat,   3
Caesar to Antony. Let the old ruffian know
I have many other ways to die; meantime
Laugh at his challenge.
     Maecenas.   Caesar must think
When one so great begins to rage, he's hunted   7
Even to falling. Give him no breath, but now
Make boot of his distraction: never anger
Made good guard for itself.
     Caesar.   Let our best heads know
That tomorrow the last of many battles   11
We mean to fight. Within our files there are,
Of those that serv'd Mark Antony but late,
Enough to fetch him in. See it done,
And feast the army; we have store to do't,   15
And they have earn'd the waste. Poor Antony!
                                         Exeunt.

Enter Antony, Cleopatra, Enobarbus, Charmian,
Iras, Alexas, with others.

Antony. He will not fight with me, Domitius?
Enobarbus.   No.
Antony. Why should he not?

SD **Enter Caesar** begins IV.1. 9 **Make boot** take advantage. 14
fetch him in capture him (surround him). SD **Enter Antony** begins
IV.2.

Enobarbus. He thinks, being twenty times of better
    fortune,
He is twenty men to one.
  Antony.   Tomorrow, soldier,   4
By sea and land I'll fight: or I will live,
Or bathe my dying honor in the blood
Shall make it live again. Woo't thou fight well?   7
  Enobarbus. I'll strike, and cry 'Take all.'
  Antony.   Well said; come on
Call forth my household servants; let's tonight
Be bounteous at our meal.

        Enter three or four Servitors.

                    Give me thy hand,
Thou hast bin rightly honest, so hast thou,   11
Thou, and thou, and thou: you have serv'd me well,
And kings have been your fellows.
  Cleopatra.   What means this?
  Enobarbus. 'Tis one of those odd tricks which sor-
    row shoots
Out of the mind.
  Antony.   And thou art honest too.
I wish I could be made so many men,   16
And all of you clapp'd up together in
An Antony, that I might do you service
So good as you have done.
  Omnes.   The gods forbid!   19
  Antony. Well, my good fellows, wait on me tonight:
Scant not my cups, and make as much of me
As when mine empire was your fellow too,
And suffer'd my command.
  Cleopatra.   What does he mean?

5 or either. 7 Woo't wilt. 8 'Take all' N. 19 Omnes i.e. servants.
23 suffer'd submitted to.

Enobarbus. To make his followers weep.

Antony.   Tend me tonight;
May be it is the period of your duty: 25
Haply, you shall not see me more, or if,
A mangled shadow. Perchance tomorrow
You'll serve another master. I look on you   28
As one that takes his leave. Mine honest friends,
I turn you not away, but like a master
Married to your good service, stay till death:
Tend me tonight two hours, I ask no more,   32
And the gods yield you for't!

Enobarbus.   What mean you, sir,
To give them this discomfort? Look, they weep,
And I, an ass, am onion-ey'd; for shame,
Transform us not to women.

Antony.   Ho, ho, ho!   36
Now, the witch take me, if I meant it thus!
Grace grow where those drops fall! My hearty
        friends,
You take me in too dolorous a sense,   39
For I spake to you for your comfort, did desire you
To burn this night with torches. Know, my hearts,
I hope well of tomorrow, and will lead you
Where rather I'll expect victorious life
Than death and honor. Let's to supper, come,   44
And drown consideration.   *Exeunt.*

Enter a company of Soldiers.

1. Soldier. Brother, good night: tomorrow is the
        day.

24 **Tend** wait on. 25 **period** end. 26 **Haply** very likely. 33 **yield**
repay, reward. 38 **Grace** virtue. 40 **comfort** encouragement.
SD **Enter a company** begins IV.3. 1–24 **Brother . . . 'Tis strange**
N.

2. Soldier. It will determine one way: fare you well.
Heard you of nothing strange about the streets?

1. Soldier. Nothing. What news?   4

2. Soldier. Belike 'tis but a rumor. Good night to
you.

1. Soldier. Well, sir, good night.

They meet other Soldiers.

2. Soldier. Soldiers, have careful watch.

3. Soldier. And you. Good night, good night.   8

*They place themselves in every
corner of the stage.*

4. Soldier. Here we: and if tomorrow
Our navy thrive, I have an absolute hope
Our landmen will stand up.

3. Soldier.   'Tis a brave army,   11
And full of purpose.

Music of the hautboys is under the stage.

4. Soldier.   Peace! what noise?

1. Soldier.   List, list!

2. Soldier. Hark!

1. Soldier.   Music i' th' air.

3. Soldier.   Under the earth.

4. Soldier. It signs well, does it not?

3. Soldier.   No.

1. Soldier.   Peace, I say!
What should this mean?

2. Soldier. 'Tis the god Hercules, whom Antony
lov'd,   16
Now leaves him.

5 Belike very likely. 8, 11 **3. Soldier** F *1.* 9, 12 **4. Soldier** F *2;*
l. 14, *4.* 11 **brave** splendid. 14 **It signs well** it is a good omen.
16 **'Tis . . . Hercules** N.

1. Soldier.   Walk; let's see if other watchmen
Do hear what we do.
2. Soldier.   How now, masters!
                    [*They*] *speak together.*
Omnes. How now? How now? Do you hear this?
1. Soldier. Ay; is't not strange?   20
3. Soldier. Do you hear, masters? do you hear?
1. Soldier. Follow the noise so far as we have
     quarter.
Let's see how it will give off.
Omnes. Content. 'Tis strange.   *Exeunt.*

Enter Antony and Cleopatra, with others.

Antony. Eros! mine armor, Eros!
Cleopatra.   Sleep a little.
Antony. No, my chuck. Eros, come; mine armor,
     Eros.

Enter Eros [with armor].

Come, good fellow, put thine iron on:
If fortune be not ours today, it is   4
Because we brave her. Come.
Cleopatra.   Nay, I'll help too.
What's this for?
Antony.   Ah, let be, let be; thou art
The armorer of my heart: false, false; this, this.
Cleopatra. Sooth—la, I'll help: thus it must be.   8
Antony. Well, well, we shall thrive now.
Seest thou, my good fellow? Go, put on thy defenses.
Eros. Briefly, sir.

---

18 masters gentlemen. 22 so far . . . quarter to the limits of our
post. 23 give off end. SD Enter Antony begins IV.4. 2 chuck
chick. 5–8 Nay . . . must be. N. 7 false wrong. 8 Sooth in truth.

Cleopatra.　　Is not this buckled well?
Antony.　　　　　　　　Rarely, rarely:
He that unbuckles this, till we do please　　12
To daff't for our repose, shall hear a storm.
Thou fumblest, Eros, and my queen's a squire
More tight at this than thou: dispatch. O love,
That thou couldst see my wars today, and knew'st
The royal occupation, thou shouldst see　　17
A workman in't.

Enter an armed Soldier.

　　　　　　Good morrow to thee; welcome;
Thou look'st like him that knows a warlike charge:
To business that we love we rise betime,　　20
And go to't with delight.
　Soldier. A thousand, sir, early though't be, have on
　　their
Riveted trim, and at the port expect you.
　　　　　　　　Shout. Trumpets flourish.

Enter Captains and Soldiers.

Captain. The morn is fair. Good morrow, general.
All. Good morrow, general.
Antony.　　　　　　　'Tis well blown, lads.　25
This morning, like the spirit of a youth
That means to be of note, begins betimes.
So, so; come, give me that: this way; well said.　28
Fare thee well, dame; whatere becomes of me
This is a soldier's kiss: [*Kisses her.*] rebukable
And worthy shameful check it were, to stand

13 daff't doff it, put it off; F *daft.* 15 tight able. 18 workman
expert craftsman. 19 charge duty. 20 betime early. 23 Riveted
trim armor. port gate. 24 Captain F *Alexas.* 25 'Tis well blown
the day begins (blossoms) well. 28 well said well done; F *well-sed.*
31 check reproof.

On more mechanic compliment. I'll leave thee   **32**
Now like a man of steel. You that will fight,
Follow me close; I'll bring you to't. Adieu.
       Exeunt [all but Cleopatra and Charmian].
Charmian. Please you, retire to your chamber.
Cleopatra.   Lead me.
He goes forth gallantly. That he and Caesar might
Determine this great war in single fight!   **37**
Then, Antony—but now—Well, on.   *Exeunt.*

    Trumpets sound. Enter Antony and Eros
        [a Soldier meeting them].

Soldier. The gods make this a happy day to Antony!
Antony. Would thou and those thy scars had once
    prevail'd
To make me fight at land!
Soldier.   Hadst thou done so,
The kings that have revolted and the soldier   **4**
That has this morning left thee would have still
Follow'd thy heels.
Antony.   Who's gone this morning?
Soldier.   Who?
One ever near thee: call for Enobarbus,
He shall not hear thee, or from Caesar's camp   **8**
Say, 'I am none of thine.'
Antony. What sayst thou?
Soldier.   Sir, he is with Caesar.
Eros. Sir, his chests and treasure he has not with
    him.
Antony. Is he gone?   **12**
Soldier. Most certain.
Antony. Go, Eros, send his treasure after; do it;

---

32 **mechanic compliment** vulgar, common **leave-taking. SD**
Trumpets sound begins IV.5. 1, 3, 6 **Soldier** N.

Detain no jot, I charge thee: write to him—
I will subscribe—gentle adieus and greetings;   10
Say that I wish he never find more cause
To change a master. O, my fortunes have
Corrupted honest men! Dispatch. Enobarbus!
                                        [*Exeunt.*]

*Flourish. Enter Agrippa, Caesar, with Enobarbus
and Dolabella.*

  Caesar. Go forth, Agrippa, and begin the fight: 20
Our will is Antony be took alive;
Make it so known.
  Agrippa.   Caesar, I shall.   [*Exit.*]
  Caesar. The time of universal peace is near:
Prove this a prosp'rous day, the three-nook'd world
Shall bear the olive freely.   25

Enter a Messenger.

  Messenger. Antony is come into the field.
  Caesar. Go charge Agrippa
Plant those that have revolted in the vant,   28
That Antony may seem to spend his fury
Upon himself.   *Exeunt* [*Caesar and his train*].
  Enobarbus. Alexas did revolt, and went to Jewry on
Affairs of Antony; there did dissuade
Great Herod to incline himself to Caesar,   32
And leave his master Antony: for this pains
Caesar hath hang'd him. Canidius and the rest
That fell away have entertainment, but
No honorable trust. I have done ill,   36

SD [Exeunt] F *Exit.* SD Flourish N. 24 **three-nook'd** three-
cornered (Europe, Asia, Africa). 28 **vant** vaunt, van. 30–4 **Alexas
. . . him** N. 31 **dissuade** persuade away from. 35 **have entertainment** are employed (in Caesar's army).

Of which I do accuse myself so sorely
That I will joy no more.

Enter a Soldier of Caesar's

Soldier. Enobarbus, Antony
Hath after thee sent all thy treasure, with   40
His bounty overplus. The messenger
Came on my guard, and at my tent is now
Unloading of his mules.

Enobarbus.   I give it you.

Soldier. Mock not, Enobarbus,   44
I tell you true: best you saf'd the bringer
Out of the host. I must attend mine office,
Or would have done't myself. Your emperor   47
Continues still a Jove.   *Exit.*

Enobarbus. I am alone the villain of the earth,
And feel I am so most. O Antony,
Thou mine of bounty, how wouldst thou have paid
My better service, when my turpitude   52
Thou dost so crown with gold! This blows my heart:
If swift thought break it not, a swifter mean
Shall outstrike thought; but thought will do't, I feel.
I fight against thee! No: I will go seek   56
Some ditch, wherein to die; the foul'st best fits
My latter part of life.   *Exit.*

Alarum. Drums and trumpets. Enter Agrippa.

Agrippa. Retire, we have engag'd ourselves too far.
Caesar himself has work, and our oppression   60
Exceeds what we expected.   *Exit.*

42 **on my guard** while I was on guard. 45 **saf'd** conducted safely.
46 **office** duty. 53 **blows** causes it to swell (with pain). 55 **outstrike**
strike sooner. **thought** sorrow, grief. SD **Alarum** N. 59 **engag'd
. . . far** involved ourselves too deeply in enemy's forces. 60 **our
oppression** pressure on us.

Alarums. Enter Antony, and Scarus wounded.

Scarus. O my brave emperor, this is fought indeed!
Had we done so at first, we had droven them home
With clouts about their heads.
   Antony.   Thou bleed'st apace.
Scarus. I had a wound here that was like a *T*,   65
But now 'tis made an *H*.
                  [Retreat sounded a]far off.
Antony.   They do retire.
Scarus. We'll beat 'em into bench holes. I have yet
Room for six scotches more.   68

Enter Eros.

Eros. They are beaten, sir, and our advantage
   serves
For a fair victory.
   Scarus.   Let us score their backs,
And snatch 'em up as we take hares behind:
'Tis sport to maul a runner.
   Antony.   I will reward thee   72
Once for thy sprightly comfort and tenfold
For thy good valor. Come thee on.
   Scarus.   I'll halt after.
                              Exeunt.

Alarum. Enter Antony again in a march;
Scarus, with others.

Antony. We have beat him to his camp: run one
   before
And let the queen know of our gests. Tomorrow,

63 we had read 'we'd.' 65–6 a **T** . . . an **H** N. 66 **Retreat
sounded** F *Far off* after *heads*, l. 64. 67 bench holes privy holes.
68 scotches slashes. 74 halt limp. SD **Alarum** begins IV.6 N.
2 gests exploits; F *guests.*

Before the sun shall see's, we'll spill the blood
That has today escap'd. I thank you all,   4
For doughty-handed are you, and have fought
Not as you serv'd the cause, but as't had been
Each man's like mine; you have shown all Hectors.
Enter the city, clip your wives, your friends,   8
Tell them your feats, whilst they with joyful tears
Wash the congealment from your wounds, and kiss
The honor'd gashes whole.

Enter Cleopatra.

                    [*To Scarus.*] Give me thy hand.
To this great fairy I'll commend thy acts,   12
Make her thanks bless thee. O thou day o' th' world!
Chain mine arm'd neck; leap thou, attire and all,
Through proof of harness to my heart, and there
Ride on the pants triumphing.
  Cleopatra.   Lord of lords!   16
O infinite virtue! com'st thou smiling from
The world's great snare uncaught?
  Antony.   My nightingale,
We have beat them to their beds. What, girl! though
    gray
Do something mingle with our younger brown, yet
    ha' we   20
A brain that nourishes our nerves, and can
Get goal for goal of youth. Behold this man;

7 **shown** shown yourselves. 8 **clip** embrace. 12 **fairy** enchantress.
13 **O thou . . . world** thou light-giver to the world (likening
Cleopatra to the sun). 15 **proof of harness** armor of proof. 16
triumphing stressed — —′ —. 17 **virtue** valor. 18 **My** F *Mine.*
19 **We have** read 'we've.' 21 **nerves** sinews. 22 **Get goal . . .**
youth win as many points from youth as they from us.

Commend unto his lips thy favoring hand:
Kiss it, my warrior: he hath fought today   24
As if a god, in hate of mankind, had
Destroy'd in such a shape.

 Cleopatra.   I'll give thee, friend,
An armor all of gold; it was a king's.

 Antony. He has deserv'd it, were it carbuncl'd   28
Like holy Phoebus' car. Give me thy hand:
Through Alexandria make a jolly march;
Bear our hack'd targets like the men that owe them.
Had our great palace the capacity   32
To camp this host, we all would sup together
And drink carouses to the next day's fate,
Which promises royal peril. Trumpeters,
With brazen din blast you the city's ear,   36
Make mingle with our rattling tabourines,
That heaven and earth may strike their sounds to-
  gether,
Applauding our approach.   *Exeunt.*

Enter a Sentry and his company; Enobarbus follows.

 Sentry. If we be not reliev'd within this hour,
We must return to th' court of guard: the night
Is shiny, and they say we shall embattle
By th' second hour i' th' morn.   4

 1. Watch. This last day was a shrewd one to's.

 Enobarbus. O, bear me witness, night—

 2. Watch. What man is this?

 1. Watch.   Stand close and list him.

 Enobarbus. Be witness to me, O thou blessed moon,

23 **Commend** commit. **favoring** F *sauouring.* 29 **Phoebus' car**
chariot of the sun. 31 **targets** shields. **owe** own. SD **Enter a
Sentry** begins IV.7 N. 2 **court of guard** guardroom. 3 **embattle**
draw up in battle array. 5 **shrewd** wicked. 7 **close** in concealment

102

When men revolted shall upon record   9
Bear hateful memory: poor Enobarbus did
Before thy face repent!
  Sentry.   Enobarbus!
  2. Watch. Peace: hark further.   12
  Enobarbus. O sovereign mistress of true melancholy,
The poisonous damp of night disponge upon me,
That life, a very rebel to my will,
May hang no longer on me. Throw my heart   16
Against the flint and hardness of my fault,
Which, being dried with grief, will break to powder,
And finish all foul thoughts. O Antony!
Nobler than my revolt is infamous   20
Forgive me in thine own particular,
But let the world rank me in register
A master leaver and a fugitive.
O Antony! O Antony!   [*Dies.*]
  1. Watch.   Let's speak to him.   24
  Sentry. Let's hear him, for the things he speaks
May concern Caesar.
  2. Watch.   Let's do so. But he sleeps.
  Sentry. Swoonds rather, for so bad a prayer as his
Was never yet for sleep.
  1. Watch.   Go we to him.   28
  2. Watch. Awake, sir, awake, speak to us.
  1. Watch.   Hear you, sir?
  Sentry. The hand of death hath raught him.
                   Drums afar off.
Hark! the drums demurely wake the sleepers.

9 record stressed — —'. 14 disponge squeeze out. 18 dried with
grief N. 21 in . . . particular yourself. 22 in register in its
record of human conduct. 23 master leaver runaway servant.
27 Swoonds swoons. 30 raught reached, seized. 31 demurely with
subdued sound.

Let us bear him to the court of guard: he is of note.
Our hour is fully out.   33
    2. Watch. Come on, then; he may recover yet.
                                                    Exeunt.

        Enter Antony and Scarus, with their army.

    Antony. Their preparation is today by sea;
We please them not by land.
    Scarus.   For both, my lord.
    Antony. I would they'ld fight i' th' fire or i' th' air;
We'ld fight there too. But this it is; our foot   4
Upon the hills adjoining to the city
Shall stay with us. Order for sea is given,
They have put forth the haven,
Where their appointment we may best discover   8
And look on their endeavor.   *Exeunt.*

            Enter Caesar and his army.

    Caesar. But being charg'd, we will be still by land.
Which, as I take't, we shall; for his best force
Is forth to man his galleys. To the vales,   12
And hold our best advantage!   *Exeunt.*

            Enter Antony and Scarus.

    Antony. Yet they are not join'd.
Where yond pine does stand, I shall discover all.
I'll bring thee word straight how 'tis like to go.   16
                                                    Exit.

    Scarus. Swallows have built
In Cleopatra's sails their nests. The augurers

SD **Enter Antony** begins IV.8 N. 8 **appointment** nature and de-
ployment of their ships. SD **Enter Caesar** N. 10 **still** quiet. 11
shall i.e. remain quiet. SD **Enter Antony** N. 14 **join'd** joined in
battle. 17–20 **Swallows . . . knowledge** N. 18 **augurers** F *Au-*
guries.
            104

Say they know not, they cannot tell, look grimly,
And dare not speak their knowledge. Antony   20
Is valiant and dejected, and by starts
His fretted fortunes give him hope and fear
Of what he has and has not.

              Alarum afar off, as at a sea fight.

              Enter Antony.

Antony.   All is lost!
This foul Egyptian hath betrayed me: 24
My fleet hath yielded to the foe, and yonder
They cast their caps up and carouse together
Like friends long lost. Triple-turn'd whore! 'tis thou
Hast sold me to this novice, and my heart   28
Makes only wars on thee. Bid them all fly:
For when I am reveng'd upon my charm,
I have done all. Bid them all fly, be gone.

                        [Exit Scarus.]

O sun! thy uprise shall I see no more;   32
Fortune and Antony part here, even here
Do we shake hands. All come to this? The hearts
That spaniel'd me at heels, to whom I gave
Their wishes, do discandy, melt their sweets   36
On blossoming Caesar; and this pine is bark'd,
That overtopp'd them all. Betray'd I am.
O this false soul of Egypt! this grave charm,
Whose eye beck'd forth my wars, and call'd them
     home,   40
Whose bosom was my crownet, my chief end,

22 **fretted** checkered, varied. SD **Alarum . . . fight** F prints at
end of l. 13. 27 **Triple-turn'd** Julius Caesar's, Cneius Pompey's,
and Antony's mistress. 30 **charm** enchantress. 35 **spaniel'd** F
panelled. 36 **discandy** dissolve. 39 **grave charm** evil-working enchantress. 40 **beck'd** beckoned. 41 **my crownet, my chief end** N.

Like a right gypsy hath at fast and loose
Beguil'd me to the very heart of loss.
What, Eros! Eros!

Enter Cleopatra.

                 Ah, thou spell! Avaunt!   44
Cleopatra. Why is my lord enrag'd against his
   love?
Antony. Vanish, or I shall give thee thy deserving,
And blemish Caesar's triumph. Let him take thee,
And hoist thee up to the shouting plebians;   48
Follow his chariot, like the greatest spot
Of all thy sex. Most monsterlike, be shown
For poor'st diminitives, for dolts, and let
Patient Octavia plough thy visage up   52
With her prepared nails.   *Exit Cleopatra.*
             'Tis well th' art gone,
If it be well to live; but better 'twere
Thou fell'st into my fury, for one death
Might have prevented many. Eros, ho!   56
The shirt of Nessus is upon me; teach me,
Alcides, thou mine ancestor, thy rage.
Let me lodge Lichas on the horns o' th' moon,
And with those hands that grasp'd the heaviest club
Subdue my worthiest self. The witch shall die.   61
To the young Roman boy she hath sold me, and I fall
Under this plot; she dies for't. Eros, ho!   *Exit.*

Enter Cleopatra, Charmian, Iras, [and] Mardian.

Cleopatra. Help me, my women! O, he's more mad

42 right true. 43 loss ruin. 44 **Avaunt!** be gone! 51 **diminitives**
diminutives; undersized, weak creatures. **dolts** fools N. 57 **shirt
of Nessus** N. 58 **Alcides** Hercules. 61 **worthiest** noblest. 62 **she
hath** read 'she'th.' SD **Enter Cleopatra** begins IV.9. 1 **he's** read
'he is.'

Than Telamon for his shield; the boar of Thessaly
Was never so emboss'd.

   Charmian. To th' monument! There lock yourself,
And send him word you are dead.   5
The soul and body rive not more in parting
Than greatness going off.

   Cleopatra.   To th' monument!
Mardian, go tell him I have slain myself;   8
Say that the last I spoke was 'Antony,'
And word it, prithee, piteously. Hence, Mardian,
And bring me how he takes my death. To th' monu-
     ment!   *Exeunt.*

Enter Antony and Eros.

   Antony. Eros, thou yet behold'st me?
   Eros.   Ay, noble lord.
   Antony. Sometime we see a cloud that's dragonish,
A vapor sometime like a bear or lion,
A tower'd citadel, a pendant rock,   4
A forked mountain, or blue promontory
With trees upon't, that nod unto the world
And mock our eyes with air: thou hast seen these
     signs;
They are black vesper's pageants.

   Eros.   Ay, my lord.
   Antony. That which is now a horse, even with a
     thought
The rack dislimns, and makes it indistinct,
As water is in water.

   Eros.   It does, my lord.

2 Telamon N. boar of Thessaly N. 3 emboss'd enraged, foaming
at the mouth. 4 To th' monument N. 6 rive rend. SD **Enter
Antony** begins IV.10. 8 **black . . . pageants** N. 9 even read
'e'en.' 10 **rack** drifting cloud. dislimns unpaints, paints out

Antony. My good knave, Eros, now thy captain is
Even such a body: here I am Antony,   13
Yet cannot hold this visible shape, my knave.
I made these wars for Egypt, and the queen—
Whose heart I thought I had, for she had mine,   16
Which whilst it was mine had annex'd unto't
A million moe, now lost—she, Eros, has
Pack'd cards with Caesar, and false-play'd my glory
Unto an enemy's triumph.   20
Nay, weep not, gentle Eros; there is left us
Ourselves to end ourselves.

Enter Mardian.

O, thy vilde lady; she has robb'd me of my sword.
Mardian. No, Antony,   24
My mistress lov'd thee, and her fortunes mingl'd
With thine entirely.
Antony. Hence, saucy eunuch, peace. She hath be-
      tray'd me
And shall die the death.   28
Mardian. Death of one person can be paid but once,
And that she has discharg'd. What thou wouldst do
Is done unto thy hand: the last she spake
Was 'Antony! most noble Antony!'   32
Then in the midst a tearing groan did break
The name of Antony; it was divided
Between her heart and lips: she rend'red life,
Thy name so buried in her.
Antony.   Dead, then?
Mardian.   Dead.   36
Antony. Unarm, Eros, the long day's task is done,

12 knave fellow. 15 Egypt the Queen of Egypt. 18 moe more.
19–20 Pack'd . . . triumph N. 23 vilde vile. sword soldierly
strength and courage. 35 rend'red gave up.

And we must sleep. [*To Mardian.*] That thou de-
    part'st hence safe,
Does pay thy labor richly; go.   *Exit Mardian.*
                     Off, pluck off:
The sevenfold shield of Ajax cannot keep   40
The battery from my heart. O, cleave, my sides!
Heart, once be stronger than thy continent,
Crack thy frail case! Apace, Eros, apace.
No more a soldier: bruised pieces, go;   44
You have bin nobly borne. From me awhile.
                         Exit Eros.
I will o'retake thee, Cleopatra, and
Weep for my pardon. So it must be, for now
All length is torture: since the torch is out,   48
Lie down and stray no farther. Now all labor
Mars what it does; yea, very force entangles
Itself with strength: seal then, and all is done.
Eros!—I come, my queen. Eros! Stay for me.   52
Where souls do couch on flowers, we'll hand in hand,
And with our sprightly port make the ghosts gaze:
Dido and her Aeneas shall want troops,
And all the haunt be ours. Come, Eros! Eros!   56

Enter Eros.

Eros. What would my lord?
  Antony.   Since Cleopatra died,
I have liv'd in such dishonor that the gods
Detest my baseness. I, that with my sword
Quarter'd the world, and o're green Neptune's back
With ships made cities, condemn myself to lack   61

42 **thy continent** thy case, that which holds thee in. 48 **length**
prolongation of life. 51 **seal** put the seal of death upon. 54 **port**
bearing. 55 **want troops** lack admirers among the departed souls.
56 **all . . . ours** we shall be the center of attraction there. 61 **to
lack** in that I lack.

The courage of a woman, less noble mind
Than she which by her death our Caesar tells
'I am conqueror of myself.' Thou art sworn, Eros,
That when the exigent should come—which now   65
Is come indeed—when I should see behind me
Th' inevitable prosecution of disgrace and horror,
That on my command thou then wouldst kill me.   68
Do't, the time is come. Thou strik'st not me,
'Tis Caesar thou defeat'st. Put color in thy cheek.
 Eros. The gods withhold me!
Shall I do that which all the Parthian darts,   72
Though enemy, lost aim and could not?
 Antony.   Eros,
Wouldst thou be window'd in great Rome and see
Thy master thus with pleach'd arms, bending down
His corrigible neck, his face subdu'd   76
To penetrative shame, whilst the wheel'd seat
Of fortunate Caesar, drawn before him, branded
His baseness that ensu'd?
 Eros.   I would not see't.
 Antony. Come, then; for with a wound I must be
  cur'd.   80
Draw that thy honest sword, which thou hast worn
Most useful for thy country.
 Eros.   O, sir! pardon me.
 Antony. When I did make thee free, swor'st thou
  not then
To do this when I bade thee? Do't at once,   84
Or thy precedent services are all

65 **exigent** emergency. 67 **inevitable prosecution** unavoidable
pursuit. 70 **defeat'st** frustratest. 75 **pleach'd** folded. 76 **corrigible**
submissive. 77 **penetrative** penetrating. 79 **His baseness that**
ensu'd the baseness of one who (as captive) followed (the chariot).
81 **honest** honorable. 85 **precedent** former.

But accidents unpurpos'd. Draw and come.

Eros. Turn from me then that noble countenance
Wherein the worship of the whole world lies.   88

Antony. Lo thee!

Eros. My sword is drawn.

Antony.   Then let it do at once
The thing why thou hast drawn it.

Eros.   My dear master,
My captain, and my emperor, let me say,   92
Before I strike this bloody stroke, farewell.

Antony. 'Tis said, man, and farewell.

Eros. Farewell, great chief. Shall I strike now?

Antony. Now, Eros.   96

Eros. Why there then.
Thus do I escape the sorrow of Antony's death.

                              Kills himself.

Antony. Thrice-nobler than myself!
Thou teachest me, O valiant Eros, what   100
I should, and thou couldst not. My queen and Eros
Have by their brave instruction got upon me
A nobleness in record; but I will be
A bridegroom in my death, and run into't   104
As to a lover's bed. Come, then; and, Eros,
Thy master dies thy scholar: to do thus

                    [*Falls on his sword.*]

I learn'd of thee. How! not dead? not dead?
The guard, ho! O, dispatch me!   108

        Enter [Dercetas and] guard.

1. Guard. What's the noise?

Antony.   I have done my work ill, friends.

SD **Kills himself** F prints SD after *Eros*, l. 96. 102–3 **Have . . .
record** have won from me a noble position in history. 108 **ho!**
F *how?* SD **Enter [Dercetas and]** N.

111

O, make an end of what I have begun.

2. Guard. The star is fall'n.

1. Guard.   And time is at his period.

All. Alas, and woe!

Antony.   Let him that loves me strike me dead.

1. Guard. Not I.   113

2. Guard. Nor I.

3. Guard. Nor any one.   *Exeunt [Guards].*

Dercetas. Thy death and fortunes bid thy followers
    fly.   116
This sword but shown to Caesar, with this tidings,
Shall enter me with him.

Enter Diomedes.

Diomedes. Where's Antony?

Dercetas.   There, Diomed, there.

Diomedes. Lives he? Wilt thou not answer, man?
                               [Exit Dercetas.]

Antony. Art thou there, Diomed? Draw thy sword,
    and give me   121
Sufficing strokes for death.

Diomedes.   Most absolute lord,
My mistress Cleopatra sent me to thee.

Antony. When did she send thee?

Diomedes.   Now, my lord.

Antony.   Where is she?

Diomedes. Lock'd in her monument. She had a
    prophesying fear   125
Of what hath come to pass: for when she saw—
Which never shall be found—you did suspect
She had dispos'd with Caesar, and that your rage

---

111 **period** end. 118 **Shall . . . him** will successfully recommend
me to him. 127 **found** found true. 128 **dispos'd** come to terms.
   112

Would not be purg'd, she sent you word she was
    dead;   129
But fearing since how it might work hath sent
Me to proclaim the truth, and I am come,
I dread, too late.   132
    Antony. Too late, good Diomed. Call my guard, I
        prithee.
    Diomedes. What, ho! the emperor's guard!
The guard, what ho! Come, your lord calls!

    Enter four or five of the guard of Antony.

    Antony. Bear me, good friends, where Cleopatra
        bides;   136
'Tis the last service that I shall command you.
    1. Guard. Woe, woe are we, sir, you may not live
        to wear
All your true followers out.
    All.   Most heavy day!
    Antony. Nay, good my fellows, do not please sharp
        fate   140
To grace it with your sorrows. Bid that welcome
Which comes to punish us, and we punish it
Seeming to bear it lightly. Take me up;
I have led you oft; carry me now, good friends,   144
And have my thanks for all.
                            Exeunt, bearing Antony.

*Enter Cleopatra and her maids aloft, with Charmian
        and Iras.*

    Cleopatra. O Charmian, I will never go from hence.
    Charmian. Be comforted, dear madam.

---

129 purg'd cleared away, pacified. **141 To grace it** by honoring it.
SD Exeunt F *Exit.* SD **Enter Cleopatra** begins IV.11.

Cleopatra.   No, I will not.
All strange and terrible events are welcome,
But comforts we despise; our size of sorrow,   4
Proportion'd to our cause, must be as great
As that which makes it.

Enter [below] Diomedes.

                    How now? is he dead?
Diomedes. His death's upon him, but not dead.
Look out o' th' other side your monument;   8
His guard have brought him thither.

Enter [below] Antony [borne by] the guard.

Cleopatra.   O sun!
Burn the great sphere thou mov'st in; darkling stand
The varying shore o' th' world. O Antony,   11
Antony, Antony! Help, Charmian, help, Iras, help;
Help, friends below, let's draw him hither.
Antony.   Peace!
Not Caesar's valor hath o'rethrown Antony,
But Antony's hath triumph'd on itself.
Cleopatra. So it should be,   16
That none but Antony should conquer Antony,
But woe 'tis so.
Antony. I am dying, Egypt, dying; only
I here importune death awhile, until   20
Of many thousand kisses the poor last
I lay upon thy lips.
Cleopatra.   I dare not, dear,
Dear my lord, pardon: I dare not,
Lest I be taken: not th' imperious show   24
Of the full-fortun'd Caesar ever shall

10 **sphere** see III.11.147 N. **darkling** in darkness. 11 **varying**
ever changing. 24 **imperious show** imperial triumph.
    114

Be brooch'd with me, if knife, drugs, serpents have
Edge, sting, or operation. I am safe:
Your wife Octavia, with her modest eyes   28
And still conclusion, shall acquire no honor
Demuring upon me. But come, come, Antony—
Help me, my women—we must draw thee up.
Assist, good friends.

   Antony.   O, quick, or I am gone.   32

   Cleopatra. Here's sport indeed! How heavy weighs
     my lord!
Our strength is all gone into heaviness;
That makes the weight. Had I great Juno's power,
The strong-wing'd Mercury should fetch thee up
And set thee by Jove's side. Yet come a little,   37
Wishers were ever fools. O, come, come, come.

       They heave Antony aloft to Cleopatra.
And welcome, welcome! Die when thou hast liv'd,
Quicken with kissing: had my lips that power,   40
Thus would I wear them out.

   All.   A heavy sight!

   Antony. I am dying, Egypt, dying.
Give me some wine, and let me speak a little.

   Cleopatra. No, let me speak, and let me rail so high
That the false huswife Fortune break her wheel,   45
Provok'd by my offense.

   Antony.   One word, sweet queen.
Of Caesar seek your honor with your safety. O!

   Cleopatra. They do not go together.

   Antony.   Gentle, hear me:
None about Caesar trust, but Proculeius.   49

---

26 **brooch'd** adorned. 29 **still conclusion** calm inference. 34 **heaviness** play on double meaning: 'weight' and 'sorrow.' SD **They heave . . . Cleopatra** N. 39 **when** N. 40 **Quicken** revive. 45 **huswife** hussy, strumpet. 46 **Provok'd** incited.

Cleopatra. My resolution and my hands I'll trust,
None about Caesar.

   Antony. The miserable change now at my end   52
Lament nor sorrow at; but please your thoughts
In feeding them with those my former fortunes
Wherein I liv'd, the greatest prince o' th' world,
The noblest: and do now not basely die,   56
Not cowardly put off my helmet to
My countryman. A Roman by a Roman
Valiantly vanquish'd. Now my spirit is going,
I can no more.

   Cleopatra.   Noblest of men, woo't die?   60
Hast thou no care of me? shall I abide
In this dull world, which in thy absence is
No better than a sty? O, see, my women,

                                      [Antony dies.]
The crown o' th' earth doth melt. My lord!   64
O, wither'd is the garland of the war,
The soldier's pole is fall'n: young boys and girls
Are level now with men: the odds is gone,
And there is nothing left remarkable   68
Beneath the visiting moon.   *[Swoons.]*

   Charmian.   O, quietness, lady!

   Iras. She is dead too, our sovereign.

   Charmian.   Lady!

   Iras.   Madam!

   Charmian. O madam, madam, madam!

   Iras. Royal Egypt! Empress!   72

   Charmian. Peace, peace, Iras!

52–9 The miserable . . . vanquish'd N. 60 woo't wilt thou. 66
pole garlanded Maypole, central point of sports N. 67 **odds**
difference. 68 **remarkable** noteworthy, distinguished.

Cleopatra. No more, but in a woman, and com-
    manded
By such poor passion as the maid that milks
And does the meanest chares. It were for me   76
To throw my scepter at the injurious gods,
To tell them that this world did equal theirs
Till they had stol'n our jewel. All's but naught;
Patience is sottish, and impatience does   80
Become a dog that's mad: then is it sin
To rush into the secret house of death
Ere death dare come to us? How do you, women?
What, what, good cheer? Why, how now, Charmian?
My noble girls! Ah, women, women! look,   85
Our lamp is spent, it's out. Good sirs, take heart:
We'll bury him, and then, what's brave, what's noble,
Let's do't after the high Roman fashion,   88
And make death proud to take us. Come, away.
This case of that huge spirit now is cold.
Ah, women, women! Come; we have no friend
But resolution, and the briefest end.   92
        Exeunt, bearing off Antony's body.

*Enter Caesar, Agrippa, Dolabella, Maecenas,
[Gallus, Proculeius,] with his Council of War.*

  Caesar. Go to him, Dolabella, bid him yield;
Being so frustrate, tell him
He mocks the pauses that he makes.
  Dolabella. Caesar, I shall.   *[Exit.]*

Enter Dercetas, with the sword of Antony.

74 in even N. 76 **chares** chores. 80 **sottish** foolish. 86 **lamp** source
of our light. **sirs** addressed to the women. 87 **brave** fine. 88 **do't**
read 'do it.' SD **Enter Caesar** begins V.1. Instead of *Maecenas* F
prints *Menas.* 2 **frustrate** baffled. 3 **He mocks . . . makes** he
makes his own delay ridiculous.

117

Caesar. Wherefore is that? And what art thou that
    dar'st   5
Appear thus to us?
Dercetas.   I am call'd Dercetas,
Mark Antony I serv'd, who best was worthy
Best to be serv'd: whilst he stood up and spoke   8
He was my master, and I wore my life
To spend upon his haters. If thou please
To take me to thee, as I was to him
I'll be to Caesar; if thou pleasest not,   12
I yield thee up my life.
Caesar.   What is't thou sayst?
Dercetas. I say, O Caesar, Antony is dead.
Caesar. The breaking of so great a thing should
    make
A greater crack. The round world   16
Should have shook lions into civil streets,
And citizens to their dens. The death of Antony
Is not a single doom; in the name lay
A moity of the world.
Dercetas.   He is dead, Caesar;   20
Not by a public minister of justice,
Nor by a hired knife; but that self hand
Which writ his honor in the acts it did,
Hath, with the courage which the heart did lend it,
Splitted the heart. This is his sword;   25
I robb'd his wound of it; behold it stain'd
With his most noble blood.
Caesar.   Look you sad, friends?
The gods rebuke me, but it is tidings   28
To wash the eyes of kings.
Agrippa.   And strange it is,

17 **civil streets** streets of cities. 20 **moity** moiety, half. 22 **self**
selfsame. 29, 33 **Agrippa** N.

That nature must compel us to lament
Our most persisted deeds.

   Maecenas. His taints and honors wag'd equal with
      him.   32

   Agrippa. A rarer spirit never
Did steer humanity: but you, gods, will give us
Some faults to make us men. Caesar is touch'd.

   Maecenas. When such a spacious mirror's set before
      him,   36
He needs must see himself.

   Caesar.   O Antony!
I have follow'd thee to this; but we do launch
Diseases in our bodies. I must perforce
Have shown to thee such a declining day,   40
Or look on thine: we could not stall together
In the whole world. But yet let me lament
With tears as sovereign as the blood of hearts
That thou, my brother, my competitor   44
In top of all design, my mate in empire,
Friend and companion in the front of war,
The arm of mine own body and the heart   47
Where mine his thoughts did kindle, that our stars,
Unreconciliable, should divide our equalness to this.
Hear me, good friends—

               Enter an Egyptian.

But I will tell you at some meeter season:
The business of this man looks out of him;   52
We'll hear him what he says. Whence are you?

---

31 **persisted** persistently pursued. 32 **wag'd equal** were evenly
matched. 38 **launch** lance. 41 **stall** dwell. 44 **competitor** partner.
45 **top of all design** loftiest enterprise. 51 **meeter** more fitting.
52 **looks out of him** shows itself in his eyes.

Egyptian. A poor Egyptian yet. The queen my mistress,
Confin'd in all she has, her monument,
Of thy intents desires instruction,   56
That she preparedly may frame herself
To th' way she's forc'd to.
Caesar.   Bid her have good heart;
She soon shall know of us, by some of ours,
How honorable and how kindly we   60
Determine for her; for Caesar cannot live
To be ungentle.
Egyptian.   So the gods preserve thee!   *Exit.*
Caesar. Come hither, Proculeius. Go and say
We purpose her no shame: give her what comforts
The quality of her passion shall require,   65
Lest in her greatness by some mortal stroke
She do defeat us. For her life in Rome
Would be eternal in our triumph. Go,   68
And with your speediest bring us what she says,
And how you find of her.
Proculeius.   Caesar, I shall.
                                        Exit Proculeius.
Caesar. Gallus, go you along.   [*Exit Gallus.*]
                          Where's Dolabella,
To second Proculeius?
All.   Dolabella!   72
Caesar. Let him alone, for I remember now
How he's employ'd: he shall in time be ready.
Go with me to my tent, where you shall see
How hardly I was drawn into this war,   76

---

57 **frame** adapt. 61 **live** F *leaue.* 65 **passion** passionate grief.
68 **eternal** eternally recorded (in history). 72 **All** i.e. Agrippa and
Maecenas. 76 **hardly** unwillingly.
   120

How calm and gentle I proceeded still
In all my writings. Go with me, and see
What I can show in this.   *Exeunt.*

Enter Cleopatra, Charmian, Iras, and Mardian.

Cleopatra. My desolation does begin to make
A better life. 'Tis paltry to be Caesar:
Not being Fortune, he's but Fortune's knave,
A minister of her will: and it is great   4
To do that thing that ends all other deeds,
Which shackles accidents, and bolts up change,
Which sleeps, and never palates more the dung,
The beggar's nurse and Caesar's.   8

Enter Proculeius.

Proculeius. Caesar sends greeting to the Queen of
   Egypt
And bids thee study on what fair demands
Thou mean'st to have him grant thee.
   Cleopatra.   What's thy name?
   Proculeius. My name is Proculeius.
   Cleopatra.   Antony   12
Did tell me of you, bade me trust you, but
I do not greatly care to be deceiv'd,
That have no use for trusting. If your master
Would have a queen his beggar, you must tell him
That majesty, to keep decorum, must   17
No less beg than a kingdom: if he please
To give me conquer'd Egypt for my son,
He gives me so much of mine own as I   20
Will kneel to him with thanks.

78 writings dispatches (to Antony) N. SD Enter Cleopatra begins
V.2. 4 minister agent. 6 bolts up fetters. 7 never . . . dung no
longer tastes the fruits of this vile earth.

   Proculeius.   Be of good cheer;
Y'are fall'n into a princely hand, fear nothing.
Make your full reference freely to my lord,
Who is so full of grace that it flows over   24
On all that need. Let me report to him
Your sweet dependency, and you shall find
A conqueror that will pray in aid for kindness   27
Where he for grace is kneel'd to.
   Cleopatra.   Pray you, tell him
I am his fortune's vassal, and I send him
The greatness he has got. I hourly learn
A doctrine of obedience, and would gladly
Look him i' th' face.
   Proculeius.   This I'll report, dear lady.   32
Have comfort, for I know your plight is pitied
Of him that caus'd it.

            [Roman soldiers enter behind Cleopatra.]

You see how easily he may be surpris'd.
Guard her till Caesar come.   36
   Iras. Royal queen!
   Charmian. O Cleopatra! thou art taken, queen.
   Cleopatra. Quick, quick, good hands.
                           [Draws a dagger.]
   Proculeius.   Hold, worthy lady, hold!
                    [Seizes and disarms her.]
Do not yourself such wrong, who are in this   40
Reliev'd, but not betray'd.
   Cleopatra. What of death, too, that rids our dogs
     of languish?

23 **Make your** . . . **freely** N. **reference** appeal. 26 **dependency**
submission. 27 **will pray** . . . **kindness** N. **SD Roman** . . .**Cleopatra** N. **35–6 You see** . . . **come** N. **39 worthy** noble. **42
languish** sufferings.
   122

Proculeius. Cleopatra, do not abuse my master's
    bounty by
Th' undoing of yourself: let the world see   44
His nobleness well acted, which your death
Will never let come forth.
    Cleopatra.   Where art thou, death?
Come hither, come! come, come, and take a queen
Worth many babes and beggars!
    Proculeius.   O, temperance, lady.
    Cleopatra. Sir, I will eat no meat, I'll not drink, sir;
If idle talk will once be necessary,   50
I'll not sleep neither. This mortal house I'll ruín,
Do Caesar what he can. Know, sir, that I
Will not wait pinion'd at your master's court,
Nor once be chastis'd with the sober eye
Of dull Octavia. Shall they hoist me up
And show me to the shouting varletry   56
Of censuring Rome? Rather a ditch in Egypt
Be gentle grave unto me! rather on Nilus' mud
Lay me stark nak'd, and let the water flies
Blow me into abhorring! rather make   60
My country's high pyramides my gibbet,
And hang me up in chains!
    Proculeius.   You do extend
These thoughts of horror further than you shall
Find cause in Caesar.

Enter Dolabella.

Dolabella.   Proculeius,   64
What thou hast done thy master Caesar knows,
And he hath sent for thee; as for the queen,

44 **undoing** destruction. 48 **temperance** moderation. 53 **pinion'd**
with wings clipped. 54 **chastis'd** stressed —′—. 56 **varletry** rabble·
F *Varlotarie.*

I'll take her to my guard.

   Proculeius.   So, Dolabella,

It shall content me best: be gentle to her.   68

[*To Cleopatra.*] To Caesar I will speak what you
     shall please,

If you'll employ me to him.

   Cleopatra.   Say, I would die.

                          Exit Proculeius.

   Dolabella. Most noble empress, you have heard of
     me?   71

   Cleopatra. I cannot tell.

   Dolabella.   Assuredly you know me.

   Cleopatra. No matter, sir, what I have heard or
     known.

You laugh when boys or women tell their dreams;
Is't not your trick?

   Dolabella.   I understand not, madam.   75

   Cleopatra. I dreamt there was an Emperor Antony:
O, such another sleep, that I might see
But such another man.

   Dolabella.   If it might please ye—

   Cleopatra. His face was as the heavens, and therein
     stuck   79

A sun and moon, which kept their course and lighted
The little O, th' earth.

   Dolabella.   Most sovereign creature—

   Cleopatra. His legs bestrid the ocean; his rear'd
     arm

Crested the world: his voice was propertied
As all the tuned spheres, and that to friends;   84
But when he meant to quail and shake the orb,

---

81 O, th' earth F *o' th' earth.* 83 Crested surmounted. was propertied as harmonious. 85 quail terrify. orb earth.

He was as rattling thunder. For his bounty,
There was no winter in't; an autumn it was
That grew the more by reaping: his delights   88
Were dolphinlike, they show'd his back above
The element they liv'd in: in his livery
Walk'd crowns and crownets; realms and islands
    were
As plates dropp'd from his pocket.
  Dolabella.   Cleopatra—   92
  Cleopatra. Think you there was or might be such a
    man
As this I dreamt of?
  Dolabella.   Gentle madam, no.
  Cleopatra. You lie, up to the hearing of the gods.
But if there be or ever were one such,   96
It's past the size of dreaming: nature wants stuff
To vie strange forms with fancy, yet to imagine
An Antony were nature's piece 'gainst fancy,   99
Condemning shadows quite.
  Dolabella.   Hear me, good madam.
Your loss is as yourself, great; and you bear it
As answering to the weight: would I might never
O'retake pursu'd success, but I do feel,
By the rebound of yours, a grief that smites   104
My very heart at root.
  Cleopatra.   I thank you, sir.
Know you what Caesar means to do with me?
  Dolabella. I am loath to tell you what I would you
    knew.   107

87 an autumn F *an Anthony.* it was read "twas.' 88–90 his
delights . . . liv'd in N. 91 crownets coronets. 92 plates silver
coins. 96 or ever F *nor euer.* 98 To vie . . . fancy to compete
with imagination in the creation of wonderful forms. 98–100
yet . . . quite N.

Cleopatra. Nay, pray you, sir—
Dolabella.   Though he be honorable—
Cleopatra. He'll lead me then in triumph?
Dolabella. Madam, he will; I know't.

> *Flourish. Enter Proculeius, Caesar, Gallus,*
> *Maecenas, and others of his train.*

All. Make way there! Caesar!
Caesar. Which is the Queen of Egypt?   112
Dolabella. It is the emperor, madam.

>   *Cleopatra kneels.*

Caesar. Arise, you shall not kneel.
I pray you, rise, rise, Egypt.
Cleopatra. Sir, the gods will have it thus,   116
My master and my lord I must obey.
Caesar. Take to you no hard thoughts;
The record of what injuries you did us,
Though written in our flesh, we shall remember   120
As things but done by chance.
Cleopatra.   Sole sir o' th' world,
I cannot project mine own cause so well
To make it clear, but do confess I have
Been laden with like frailties which before   124
Have often sham'd our sex.
Caesar.   Cleopatra, know,
We will extenuate rather than enforce:
If you apply yourself to our intents,   127
Which towards you are most gentle, you shall find
A benefit in this change; but if you seek
To lay on me a cruelty, by taking
Antony's course, you shall bereave yourself
Of my good purposes, and put your children   132

122 **project** set forth; stressed —'—. 126 **enforce** stress (them).
131 **bereave** deprive.

126

To that destruction which I'll guard them from,
If thereon you rely. I'll take my leave.
   Cleopatra. And may through all the world: 'tis
     yours, and we,   135
Your scutcheons and your signs of conquest, shall
Hang in what place you please. Here, my good lord.
   Caesar. You shall advise me in all for Cleopatra.
   Cleopatra. [*Giving a scroll.*] This is the brief of
     money, plate, and jewels
I am possess'd of: 'tis exactly valued,   140
Not petty things admitted. Where's Seleucus?
   Seleucus. Here, madam.
   Cleopatra. This is my treasurer; let him speak, my
     lord,
Upon his peril, that I have reserv'd   144
To myself nothing. Speak the truth, Seleucus.
   Seleucus. Madam, I had rather seel my lips
Than to my peril speak that which is not.
   Cleopatra. What have I kept back?   148
   Seleucus. Enough to purchase what you have made
     known.
   Caesar. Nay, blush not, Cleopatra; I approve
Your wisdom in the deed.
   Cleopatra.   See, Caesar! O, behold
How pomp is follow'd; mine will now be yours,   152
And, should we shift estates, yours would be mine.
The ingratitude of this Seleucus does
Even make me wild. O slave, of no more trust
Than love that's hir'd. What! goest thou back? thou
     shalt   156

136 **scutcheons** armorial bearings, signs of victory. 139 **brief** list.
146 **seel** sew up; see III.11.113 N. 152 **How . . . follow'd** how
unfaithful are the servants of the great. 153 **shift estates** exchange
places. 155 **Even** read 'e'en.'

Go back, I warrant thee; but I'll catch thine eyes
Though they had wings: slave, soulless villain, dog!
O rarely base!

   Caesar.   Good queen, let us entreat you.

   Cleopatra. O Caesar! what a wounding shame is
     this,   160
That thou, vouchsafing here to visit me,
Doing the honor of thy lordliness
To one so meek, that mine own servant should
Parcel the sum of my disgraces by   164
Addition of his envy. Say, good Caesar,
That I some lady trifles have reserv'd,
Immoment toys, things of such dignity
As we greet modern friends withal; and say,   168
Some nobler token I have kept apart
For Livia and Octavia, to induce
Their mediation; must I be unfolded
With one that I have bred? The gods! it smites me
Beneath the fall I have. [*To Seleucus.*] Prithee, go
     hence,   173
Or I shall show the cinders of my spirits
Through th' ashes of my chance. Wert thou a man,
Thou wouldst have mercy on me.

   Caesar.   Forbear, Seleucus.

   Cleopatra. Be it known that we, the greatest, are
     misthought   177
For things that others do; and, when we fall,
We answer others' merits in our name,
Are therefore to be pitied.

---

164 **Parcel the sum** add to the sum total. 166 **lady** feminine. 167
Immoment valueless. **dignity** value. 168 **modern** ordinary. 170
Livia Octavius Caesar's wife. 171 **unfolded** betrayed. 172 **With** by.
175 **chance** fortune. 177 **misthought** misjudged. 179 **merits in
our name** faults committed in our name.

Caesar.   Cleopatra,   180
Not what you have reserv'd, nor what acknowledg'd,
Put we i' th' roll of conquest: still be't yours,
Bestow it at your pleasure, and believe
Caesar's no merchant to make prize with you   184
Of things that merchants sold. Therefore be cheer'd,
Make not your thoughts your prisons: no, dear
      queen,
For we intend so to dispose you as
Yourself shall give us counsel. Feed, and sleep: 188
Our care and pity is so much upon you
That we remain your friend; and so, adieu.
Cleopatra. My master, and my lord!
Caesar.   Not so. Adieu.
            Flourish. Exeunt Caesar and his train.
Cleopatra. He words me, girls, he words me,   192
That I should not be noble to myself;
But, hark thee, Charmian.   [*Whispers.*]
Iras. Finish, good lady, the bright day is done,
And we are for the dark.
Cleopatra.   Hie thee again: 196
I have spoke already, and it is provided;
Go, put it to the haste.
Charmian.   Madam, I will.

                Enter Dolabella.

Dolabella. Where is the queen?
Charmian.   Behold, sir. [*Exit.*]
Cleopatra.   Dolabella!
Dolabella. Madam, as thereto sworn by your com-
      mand,   200
Which my love makes religion to obey,

183 Bestow make use of. 184 make prize bargain. 192 **words me**
tries to delude me with words.

I tell you this: Caesar through Syria
Intends his journey; and within three days
You with your children will he send before.   204
Make your best use of this. I have perform'd
Your pleasure and my promise.
   Cleopatra. Dolabella, I shall remain your debtor.
   Dolabella. I your servant.   208
Adieu, good queen; I must attend on Caesar.
   Cleopatra. Farewell, and thanks. *Exit* [*Dolabella*].
                 Now, Iras, what think'st thou?
Thou, an Egyptian puppet, shall be shown
In Rome, as well as I; mechanic slaves   212
With greasy aprons, rules, and hammers shall
Uplift us to the view; in their thick breaths,
Rank of gross diet, shall we be enclouded
And forc'd to drink their vapor.
   Iras.   The gods forbid!
   Cleopatra. Nay, 'tis most certain, Iras. Saucy lic-
    tors   217
Will catch at us, like strumpets, and scald rimers
Ballad us out o' tune: the quick comedians
Extemporally will stage us and present   220
Our Alexandrian revels. Antony
Shall be brought drunken forth, and I shall see
Some squeaking Cleopatra boy my greatness
I' th' posture of a whore.
   Iras.   O, the good gods!   224
   Cleopatra. Nay, that's certain.
   Iras. I'll never see't! for I am sure my nails
Are stronger than mine eyes.

---

212 **mechanic** engaged in manual labor. 218 **scald** scurvy. 219
Ballad F *Ballads.* **quick** quick-witted. 223 **Some . . . greatness**
N. 224 **posture** behavior. 226 **my** F *mine.*
   130

Cleopatra. Why, that's the way to fool their prepa- 228
    ration,
And to conquer their most absurd intents.

          Enter Charmian.

Now, Charmian.
Show me, my women, like a queen: go fetch
My best attires. I am again for Cydnus 232
To meet Mark Antony. Sirrah Iras, go.
Now, noble Charmian, we'll dispatch indeed,
And when thou hast done this chare I'll give thee
    leave
To play till doomsday. Bring our crown and all. 236
          [Exit Iras.] A noise within.
Wherefore's this noise?

          Enter a Guardsman.

  Guardsman.   Here is a rural fellow
That will not be denied your highness' presence:
He brings you figs.
  Cleopatra. Let him come in.   *Exit Guardsman.*
          What poor an instrument 240
May do a noble deed! he brings me liberty.
My resolution's plac'd, and I have nothing
Of woman in me; now from head to foot
I am marble-constant: now the fleeting moon 244
No planet is of mine.

       Enter Guardsman and Clown [bringing
          in a basket].

  Guardsman.   This is the man.
  Cleopatra. Avoid, and leave him.   *Exit Guardsman.*

235 thou **hast** read 'thou'st.' **chare** chore. 242 **plac'd** fixed. SD
Clown rustic. 246 **Avoid** withdraw.

Hast thou the pretty worm of Nilus there,
That kills and pains not? 248

Clown. Truly, I have him: but I would not be the
party that should desire you to touch him, for his
biting is immortal; those that do die of it do seldom
or never recover.

Cleopatra. Remember'st thou any that have died
on't? 254

Clown. Very many, men and women too. I heard of
one of them no longer than yesterday—a very honest
woman, but something given to lie, as a woman
should not do but in the way of honesty—how she
died of the biting of it, what pain she felt. Truly,
she makes a very good report o' th' worm; but he
that will believe all that they say shall never be saved
by half that they do: but this is most falliable, the
worm's an odd worm. 263

Cleopatra. Get thee hence; farewell.

Clown. I wish you all joy of the worm.

                  [Sets down the basket.]

Cleopatra. Farewell.

Clown. You must think this, look you, that the
worm will do his kind. 268

Cleopatra. Ay, ay; farewell.

Clown. Look you, the worm is not to be trusted but
in the keeping of wise people: for indeed there is no
goodness in the worm. 272

Cleopatra. Take thou no care, it shall be heeded.

Clown. Very good: give it nothing, I pray you, for
it is not worth the feeding.

Cleopatra. Will it eat me? 276

247 **worm** serpent. 251 **immortal** blunder for 'mortal.' 256 **honest**
respectable. 262 **falliable** he means 'infallible.' 273 **heeded**
guarded.

Clown. You must not think I am so simple but I
know the devil himself will not eat a woman: I know
that a woman is a dish for the gods, if the devil dress
her not. But, truly, these same whoreson devils do
the gods great harm in their women, for in every ten
that they make, the devils mar five.   282

Cleopatra. Well, get thee gone, farewell.

Clown. Yes, forsooth: I wish you joy o' th' worm.
                                              Exit.

[*Enter Iras, with a robe, crown, etc.*]

Cleopatra. Give me my robe, put on my crown; I
     have
Immortal longings in me. Now no more   286
The juice of Egypt's grape shall moist this lip.
Yare, yare, good Iras; quick. Methinks I hear
Antony call: I see him rouse himself
To praise my noble act. I hear him mock   290
The luck of Caesar, which the gods give men
To excuse their after wrath. Husband, I come:
Now to that name my courage prove my title!
I am fire and air; my other elements   294
I give to baser life. So, have you done?
Come then, and take the last warmth of my lips.
Farewell, kind Charmian; Iras, long farewell.
          [*Kisses them. Iras falls and dies.*]
Have I the aspic in my lips? Dost fall?   298
If thou and nature can so gently part,
The stroke of death is as a lover's pinch,
Which hurts, and is desir'd. Dost thou lie still?
If thus thou vanishest, thou tell'st the world 302
It is not worth leave-taking.

288 **Yare** quick. 291–2 **The luck . . . wrath** N. 294–5 **my other
. . . life** N. 295 **baser life** human, mortal life. 298 **aspic** asp.

Charmian. Dissolve, thick cloud and rain, that I
  may say
The gods themselves do weep.
    Cleopatra.   This proves me base:
If she first meet the curled Antony,   306
He'll make demand of her, and spend that kiss
Which is my heaven to have. Come, thou mortal
  wretch,
With thy sharp teeth this knot intrinsicate
Of life at once untie: poor venomous fool,   310
Be angry, and dispatch. O, couldst thou speak,
That I might hear thee call great Caesar ass
Unpolicied.
    Charmian.   O eastern star!
    Cleopatra.   Peace, peace!
Dost thou not see my baby at my breast,   314
That sucks the nurse asleep?
    Charmian.   O, break! O, break!
    Cleopatra. As sweet as balm, as soft as air, as
  gentle—
O Antony!—Nay, I will take thee too.   317
           [*Applying another asp to her arm.*]
What should I stay—   *Dies.*
    Charmian. In this vile world? So, fare thee well.
Now boast thee, death, in thy possession lies   320
A lass unparallel'd. Downy windows, close,
And golden Phoebus never be beheld
Of eyes again so royal! Your crown's awry;
I'll mend it, and then play—   324

      Enter the Guard, rushing in.

308 **mortal** deadly. 309 **intrinsicate** intricate. 313 **Unpolicied** un-
skilled. 319 **vile** F *wilde*. 323 **awry** F *away*. SD **rushing in** F
rustling in, and Dolabella.
    134

1. Guard. Where is the queen?

Charmian. Speak softly, wake her not.

1. Guard. Caesar hath sent—

Charmian. Too slow a messenger.

[*Applies an asp.*]

O, come apace, dispatch; I partly feel thee.

1. Guard. Approach, ho! All's not well: Caesar's
beguil'd. 328

2. Guard. There's Dolabella sent from Caesar; call
him.

1. Guard. What work is here! Charmian, is this
well done?

Charmian. It is well done, and fitting for a princess
Descended of so many royal kings. 332
Ah, soldier. *Charmian dies.*

Enter Dolabella.

Dolabella. How goes it here?

2. Guard. All dead.

Dollabella. Caesar, thy thoughts
Touch their effects in this: thyself art coming
To see perform'd the dreaded act which thou 336
So sought'st to hinder.

Enter Caesar and all his train marching.

All. A way there!—a way for Caesar!

Dolabella. O, sir, you are too sure an augurer:
That you did fear is done.

Caesar. Bravest at the last,
She level'd at our purposes, and being royal 340
Took her own way. The manner of their deaths?
I do not see them bleed.

335 **Touch their effects** find fulfillment. 339 **That** what. 340
level'd aimed, guessed.

Dolabella.   Who was last with them?

1. Guard. A simple countryman that brought her
 figs:
This was his basket.

Caesar.   Poison'd then.

1. Guard.   O Caesar! 344
This Charmian liv'd but now; she stood, and spake:
I found her trimming up the diadem
On her dead mistress; tremblingly she stood,
And on the sudden dropp'd.

Caesar.   O noble weakness! 348
If they had swallow'd poison 'twould appear
By external swelling: but she looks like sleep,
As she would catch another Antony 351
In her strong toil of grace.

Dolabella.   Here, on her breast,
There is a vent of blood, and something blown;
The like is on her arm.

1. Guard. This is an aspic's trail,
And these fig leaves have slime upon them, such 356
As th' aspic leaves upon the caves of Nile.

Caesar. Most probable
That so she died: for her physician tells me
She hath pursu'd conclusions infinite 360
Of easy ways to die. Take up her bed,
And bear her women from the monument.
She shall be buried by her Antony.
No grave upon the earth shall clip in it 364
A pair so famous. High events as these
Strike those that make them; and their story is

346 **trimming up** straightening. 352 **toil** net, snare. **grace** beauty.
353 **vent** discharge. **blown** swollen. 359–61 **for her physician . . .
die** N. 360 **conclusions** experiments. 364 **clip** embrace.
136

No less in pity than his glory which
Brought them to be lamented. Our army shall,   368
In solemn show, attend this funeral,
And then to Rome. Come, Dolabella, see
High order in this great solemnity.   *Exeunt omnes.*

FINIS

NOTES

Act I, Scene 1

10 gypsy's The word carries a double meaning here: Cleopatra
is called an Egyptian (gypsies were believed to have come from
Egypt) and also a hussy. Cf. *NED*.

12 triple pillar One of the triumvirs, on whom, as on pillars,
the world rested.

15 beggary Like other polysyllabic words (e.g. *infinite*, I.2.10;
amorous, II.2.203; etc.), it syncopates the medial unstressed
syllable when scansion so requires; such words should therefore
be read 'begg'ry,' 'inf'nite,' etc. See Helge Kökeritz, *Shakespeare's
Pronunciation* (New Haven, Yale University Press, 1953), pp.
25 ff., 283 ff.

21 scarce-bearded Octavius was then twenty-three. Cf. 'the
young man' (III.9.62), 'the boy Cæsar' (III.11.18).

52–4 all alone . . . people 'And somtime also, when he would
goe vp and downe the citie disguised like a slaue in the night,
& would peere into poore mens windowes & their shops, and
scold and brawle with them within the house: Cleopatra would
be also in a chamber maides array, & amble vp and downe the
streets with him, so that oftentimes Antonius bare away both
mockes & blowes.' North's *Plutarch* (1579), p. 983.

Act I, Scene 2

1SD Enter Enobarbus The Folio entry includes Lamprius,
Rannius, and Lucillius, all mute characters appearing nowhere
else in the play. Lamprius was probably suggested to Shakespeare by Lampryas, Plutarch's grandfather, who related to him
the anecdote of Antony's feasts. North, p. 982.

5 change . . . garlands 'Take horns (symbol of wife's un-
faithfulness) in exchange for garlands (those of marriage).' Many
editors read *charge*, 'to load,' in which case the meaning might
be: 'to load his horns with garlands, to wear garlands on his
horns.'

26 heat . . . drinking The liver being the seat of the passion

138

of love, Charmian prefers to heat her liver with wine rather than
with unrequited love.

30–1 **Herod of Jewry** Herod of Judea, who was represented as
a fierce and blustering tyrant in the old miracle plays. Charmian
prays for a son who would command such a tyrant's homage.

36 **I . . . figs** A difficult line. It may be a proverbial expression, with *figs* carrying one of several meanings, for which
see the Arden Shakespeare, ed. M. R. Ridley (London, Methuen
and Co., 1954), p. 12. Or it may be a phallic allusion, as J. D. Wilson suggests in the Cambridge Shakespeare (Cambridge, Cambridge University Press, 1950), p. 146.

67–73 **come . . . thee** The compositor mistook *Alexas* for a
speech prefix. See Appendix A, 2.

68 **Isis** Originally the Egyptian goddess of earth and fertility.

103 **Labienus** Quintus Labienus, having joined Brutus and
Cassius in 44 B.C., was by them dispatched to seek aid from
Orodes, King of Parthia. At this point he is commanding the
Parthian army jointly with Orodes' son Pacorus.

105–8 **Extended . . . lord** Thus in F. Editors normalize passage
into strict pentameter, so that the three lines end with *Euphrates,
Syria,* and *lord.*

106 **Lydia** Ancient country in western part of Asia Minor.

114–15 **Our ills . . . earing** 'Having our faults told us is as
salutary to us as ploughing is to weed-grown fields.' For a highly
suggestive analysis of the passage see Norman H. Pearson's essay
'*Antony and Cleopatra*' in *Shakespeare: Of an Age and for All
Time,* The Yale Shakespeare Festival Lectures, ed. Charles T.
Prouty, (Hamden, Conn., The Shoe String Press, 1954), pp.
138 ff.

130 **By . . . low'ring** Carried to a progressively lower place
in our estimation by the turn of the wheel of circumstance.
Cf. *King Lear*, V.3.176.

188 **Sextus Pompeius** Younger son of Pompey the Great. He
was proscribed by the triumvirs, but taking advantage of the
quarrels between Octavius and Antony he was able to seize Sicily
and command the sea.

198 **courser's hair** Horse hairs laid in stagnant water were
believed to come to life in the shape of worms or small serpents.

Act I, Scene 3

53–4 grown . . . change Ill through inactivity (peace), it would restore itself to health through blood-letting (war). 'Purge' often carries the meaning of letting blood, as in 2 *Henry IV*, IV.1.65.

63 sacred vials Bottles of tears allegedly placed in the urn of loved ones. Cf. *The Two Noble Kinsmen*, I.5.5.

68–9 By the fire . . . slime 'By the sun, which wakes to life Nile's mud' (causing spontaneous generation). Cf. II.7.27–9.

84–5 How . . . chafe How becomingly this descendant of Hercules conducts himself in his rage; how he acts the part of another Hercules Furens.

90–1 O . . . forgotten My forgetfulness is like Antony, who is the epitome of utter forgetfulness, and I have forgotten all even as I am by all forgotten.

Act I, Scene 4

6 queen of Ptolemy Cleopatra, according to Egyptian custom, had married her brother Ptolemy, whom she is said to have poisoned.

7–11 More . . . goodness Thus in F. Editors rearrange passage into regular pentameter, making the lines end with *Or, there, faults,* and *are.*

24 foils Some editors print *soils,* an unnecessary emendation since 'soils' or 'disgraces' is precisely the meaning of *foils* in the context. Cf. *NED;* F. H. Stratmann and H. Bradley, *Middle English Dictionary; The Tempest,* III.1.46.

54–5 strikes . . . resisted Is more powerful than his actual warfare if it were opposed.

56–71 When . . . lank'd not 'And therefore it was a wonderfull example to the souldiers, to see Antonius that was brought vp in all finenes and superfluitie, so easily to drinke puddle water, and eate wild frutes and rootes: and moreouer it is reported, that euen as they passed the Alpes, they did eate the barcks of trees, and such beasts, as neuer man tasted of their flesh before.' North, pp. 977–8.

Act I, Scene 5

23 demi-Atlas Antony and Caesar each carry half the globe on their shoulders; Lepidus does not count.

31 great Pompey Not Pompey the Great but his son Cneius Pompey.

36 that great med'cine The elixir which conferred immortality and changed base metals into gold: here meaning Antony.

Act II, Scene 1

2-5 Know ... for F prints passage as prose. See Appendix A, 2.

28 Lethe'd Oblivious; as if, like the dead crossing into Hades, he had drunk Lethe's water, which caused complete and utter forgetfulness.

42 His brother 'Nowe Antonius delighting in these fond and childish pastimes, verie ill newes were brought him from two places. The first from Rome, that his brother Lucius, and Fuluia his wife, fell out first betwene them selues, and afterwards fell to open warre with Caesar . . .' North, p. 983.

51-2 It only ... upon Only it is a matter of life and death for us.

Act II, Scene 2

8 would not shave't Plucking a man's beard was an invitation to quarrel. Cf. *Hamlet*, II.2.600; *King Lear*, III.7.76.

17 Hark The F spelling *Hearke* may stand for *Hark* or *Harkee*, i.e. 'Hark ye.'

55 you have to Rowe and subsequent editors emend 'you have not to,' arguing that Antony would not admit that Caesar had a more serious grievance to 'patch a quarrel' with. The insertion of *not* may obviate Antony's alleged admission, but it does not clarify the meaning of ll. 54-6. The F lines mean: 'If you insist on starting (patching) a quarrel, you cannot do so with this particular complaint inasmuch as you have more serious complaints (matter whole) to do it with.'

87-8 The honor ... it The keeping of an oath is a sacred point of honor, which I am now accused of violating.

94–6 But . . . without it As my power shall not cause me to overlook my duty, neither shall my honesty (which dictates apology) sacrifice my dignity.

96–7 Fulvia . . . here 'By them he was informed, that his wife Fuluia was the only cause of this warre: who being of a peeuish, crooked, and troublesome nature, had purposely raised this vprore in Italie, in hope thereby to withdraw him from Cleopatra.' North, pp. 983–4.

122 by the mother's side Octavia was in fact the daughter of both Caesar's parents, though Plutarch calls her his sister 'not by one mother, for she came of Ancharia, & Caesar him self afterwards of Accia.' North, p. 984.

138–9 Truths . . . truths True reports of trouble would be dismissed as mere gossip, whereas now every rumor is accepted as the truth.

178 Half . . . Caesar Maecenas and Agrippa were equally loved by Octavius.

185 Eight wild boars Lampryas, Plutarch's grandfather, had heard from one Philotas, a physician, an eye-witness account of the 'wonderfull sumptuous charge and preparation of one only supper. When he was in the kitchin, and saw a world of diuersities of meates, and amongst others, eight wilde boares rosted whole: he began to wonder at it, and sayd, sure you haue a great number of ghests to supper. The cooke fell a laughing, and answered him, no (quoth he) not many ghestes, nor aboue twelue in all.' North, p. 982.

196–224 I will . . . nature A phonetic transcription of this famous description as it was spoken in Shakespeare's day is given in Kökeritz, *Shakespeare's Pronunciation*, p. 368.

211 what they undid did They cooled the cheeks even as they made them glow with apparent warmth.

214 made . . . adornings 'Their beautiful forms bending gracefully toward her seemed like adornments to her person.' Some editors read *adorings* and interpret: 'They did her observance in the posture of adoration as if she had been Venus.'

242 infinite variety The phrase occurs in Florio's Montaigne, in a passage contrasting the weaknesses of present 'indiscreet

writers' with the excellence of Plutarch. *The Essays of Montaigne* (New York, The Modern Library, 1933), p. 108.

Act II, Scene 3

14 I see . . . tongue I have intuitive knowledge of it but cannot express it.

21–4 Thy demon . . . o'repower'd 'With Antonius there was a soothsayer or astronomer of Aegypt . . . [who] told Antonius plainly, that his fortune (which of it selfe was excellent good, and very great) was altogether bleamished, and obscured by Caesars fortune: and therefore he counselled him vtterly to leaue his company, and to get him as farre from him as he could. For thy Demon said he, (that is to say, the good angell and spirit that kepeth thee) is affraied of his: and being coragious & high when he is alone, becometh fearefull and timerous when he commeth neere vnto the other.' North, p. 985.

27–32 If . . . 'tis noble 'But in all other maner of sportes and exercises, wherein they passed the time away the one with the other: Antonius was euer inferior vnto Caesar, and alway lost, which grieued him much.' North, p. 985.

38 His cocks 'Oftentimes when they were disposed to see cockefight, or quailes that were taught to fight one with an other: Caesars cockes or quailes did euer ouercome.' North, p. 985.

39 When . . . nought When the odds are everything to nothing in my favor.

Act II, Scene 5

15–18 'Twas . . . drew up 'Antonius then threw in his line and Cleopatra straight commaunded one of her men to diue vnder water before Antonius men, and to put some old salte fish vpon his baite, like vnto those that are brought out of the contrie of Pont.' North, p. 983.

23 Philippan The sword with which Antony had triumphed over Brutus and Cassius at Philippi in 42 B.C.

26–9 Antonio's . . . here Thus in F. Some editors rearrange lines into regular pentameters, the three resulting lines ending with *villain, free, here.*

98 **Narcissus** A beautiful youth in mythology who fell in love with his own face when he saw its reflection in the water.

101 **Take . . . you** Do not be angry with me because I do not wish to offend you.

105 **That . . . sure of** Who art not what you are certain Antony is, a deceiver and a knave.

Act II, Scene 6

26 **o'recount** Antony means 'outnumber,' whereas in the following line Pompey means 'cheat.'

26–9 **At land . . . mayst** 'Afterwards when Pompeys house was put to open sale, Antonius bought it: but when they asked him money for it, he made it very straung, and was offended with them, and writeth him selfe that he would not goe with Caesar into the warres of Africk, bicause he was not well recompenced for the seruice he had done him before.' North, p. 975.

34 **to . . . fortune** If you risk war in an attempt to gain more than we offer you.

46–7 **Your . . . friendly** 'Furthermore, Sextus Pompeius had delt verie frendly with Antonius, for he had curteously receiued his mother, when she fled out of Italie with Fuluia.' North, p. 984.

55 **counts** Marks or lines, like those on tally sticks, by which Fortune has recorded her dealings with him.

Act II, Scene 7

15–17 **To be call'd . . . cheeks** Being in a position of pre-eminence but unable to dominate or exert influence is like having holes in the place of eyes, which would give a hideous appearance to the cheeks.

37 **pyramises** Lepidus' own unsteady plural. Although *pyramis* (Greek form) and even *pyrame* (taking *pyramis* or *pyramses* as a plural) were common, the plural was *pyramides*, the form Cleopatra uses below, V.2.61.

95–6 **would . . . wheels** I wish the whole world were drunk so that it might run on wheels, that is, smoothly.

97 **reels** A contraction of *revels* not, as some editors believe, 'the world's reeling.' Cf. *Hamlet*, I.4.9, where *reels* is again a

noun, that is, a contraction of *revels* not a verb. For further
comment see Kökeritz, *Shakespeare's Pronunciation*, p. 189.

131 I'll try . . . shore I'll continue the drinking match with
you on the shore.

134–8 Take heed . . . out F prints these lines as a single
speech by Enobarbus.

Act III, Scene 1

1 darting Parthia The Parthian cavalry was noted for its
arrows, and one of its favorite maneuvers was to send a shower
of them as it retreated.

4–5 Thy Pacorus . . . Crassus 'In the mean time, Ventidius
once againe ouercame Pacorus, (Orodes sonne King of Parthia)
in a battell fought in the contrie of Cyrrestica, he being come
againe with a great armie to inuade Syria: at which battell was
slaine a great number of the Parthians, & among them Pacorus,
the kings owne sonne slaine. This noble exployt as famous as
euer any was, was a full reuenge to the Romanes, of the shame
and losse they had receiued before by the death of Marcus
Crassus.' North, p. 985.

5 Roman Some editors give this and subsequent speeches the
speech heading *Silius*, who is addressed by name in l. 11.

27–9 Thou hast . . . distinction You possess discretion, without which a man's generalship confers no great distinction on him.

Act III, Scene 2

6 green-sickness Bilious hue peculiar to lovesick maidens.
Lepidus is ironically reported as lovesick for Caesar and Antony.

6 'Tis 'It' is here used contemptuously to refer to Lepidus.

12 Arabian bird The unique phoenix, believed by the ancients
to fly from Arabia to the temple of Helios in Egypt once every
five hundred years in order to bury there its father's body.

26–7 as my . . . approof Such as I would pledge my utmost
you will prove.

40 elements Perhaps more than merely a wish for favorable
weather. Caesar wishes that the four *elements* believed to constitute the whole world may be propitious to her.

48–50 **the swan's-down . . . inclines** Octavia's emotions, that is, her love of Antony and her devotion to Octavius, are as delicately balanced as a swan's-down feather on the water at the height of the flood and just before the ebb begins.

51–2 **He has . . . horse** A horse with a dark face; one with no white on it. M. R. Ridley (Arden Shakespeare) quotes *The Two Noble Kinsmen*, V.4.63, to show that the absence of a white mark indicated ill temper.

Act III, Scene 3

4–5 **That . . . have** '. . . also he tooke from other kings their lawfull realmes: (as from Antigonus King of the Iewes, whom he openly beheaded, where neuer King before had suffred like death).' North, p. 986. Another reference may be to the beheading of Cicero by Antony's men. Antony placed Cicero's head over the pulpit for orations, which was 'a fearfull and horrible sight vnto the Romanes, who thought they saw not Ciceroes face, but an image of Antonius life and disposicion.' North, p. 937.

18 **look'st** For such F forms as *look'st* (look'dst) see Kökeritz, *Shakespeare's Pronunciation*, p. 303.

30 **long or round** A long face denoted prudence and wariness; a round one foolishness, indiscretion, instability.

34 **Brown** Brown was not associated with beauty. 'Why, i' faith, methinks she's too low for a high praise, too brown for a fair praise and too little for a great praise.' *Much Ado about Nothing*, I.1.173–5.

35 **As low . . . it** A high forehead was a mark of beauty. Mercutio speaks of Rosaline's 'high forehead and her scarlet lip.' *Romeo and Juliet*, II.1.18.

Act III, Scene 4

4 **made . . . read it** Antony is suggesting that Octavius made promises as Julius Caesar had done in his own will. Here Shakespeare departs from Plutarch, who records that Octavius, taking possession of Antony's will, read and attacked it in public. Cf. North, p. 997.

Act III, Scene 5

19 that his officer Titius, Antony's lieutenant, who is reported to have slain Pompey.

Act III, Scene 6

6 my father's son Caesarion, son of Julius Caesar and Cleopatra. Octavius was adopted as a son by Julius Caesar in his will.

10 Lydia So in North. Plutarch gives *Libya*, whose King Bocchus appears in l. 71 below.

12–19 I' th' common . . . so 'For he assembled all the people in the show place, where younge men doe exercise them selues, and there vpon a high tribunall siluered, he set two chayres of gold, the one for him selfe, and the other for Cleopatra, and lower chaires for his children: then he openly published before the assembly, that first of all he did establish Cleopatra Queene of Aegypt, of Cyprvs, of Lydia, and of the lower Syria, and at that time also, Caesarion king of the same Realmes. . . . Now for Cleopatra, she did not onely weare at that time (but at all other times els when she came abroad) the apparell of the goddesse Isis, and so gaue audience vnto all her subiects, as a new Isis.' North, p. 996.

54–5 The ostentation . . . unlov'd The display of our (Caesar's) love, which (love), if not exhibited, is often thought to be unfelt.

63 Being an abstract . . . him Variously interpreted. Perhaps the most satisfactory explanation is: 'Your return being a shortcut (abstract) between him and his lust, that is the easiest way to satisfy his desires.' Some editors read *obstruct* (as substantive) and taking it to refer to Octavia interpret: 'You being an obstruction to the satisfaction of his lust.'

83 wrong led Some editors emend F reading to *wrong'd* on the doubtful theory that the compositor misread Shakespeare's 'wronged,' inserted a space and added an *l*. But Shakespeare very probably would have written 'wrongd,' which makes the compositor's misreading difficult if not impossible.

91 makes his Some editors read *make them* or *make their*.

147

But *makes* (plural) is probably what Shakespeare wrote, and its singular form may be responsible for *his*.

Act III, Scene 7

5 Is't not denounc'd Some editors retain F reading and are thereby forced to give obscure sense.

13–15 'tis said . . . war 'And Caesar sayde furthermore, that Antonius was not Maister of him selfe, but that Cleopatra had brought him beside him selfe, by her charmes and amorous poysons: and that they that should make warre with them, should be Mardian the Euenuke, Photinus, and Iras, a Woman of Cleopatraes bedchamber, that friseled her heare, and dressed her head, and Charmion, the which were those that ruled all the affaires of Antonius Empire.' North, p. 998.

61–6 O noble emperor . . . foot 'Now, as he was setting his men in order of battel, there was a Captaine, & a valliant man, that had serued Antonius in many battels & conflicts, & had all his body hacked & cut: who as Antonius passed by him, cryed vnto him, & sayd: O, noble Emperor, how commeth it to passe that you trust to these vile brittle shippes? what, doe you mistrust these woundes of myne, and this sword? let the Aegyptians & Phaenicians fight by sea, and set vs on the maine land, where we vse to conquer, or to be slayne on our feete.' North, p. 1000.

68–9 his whole action . . . on't His plan of action does not make use of his military power with greatest advantage.

81 throws forth Most editors read *throes forth* (an extremely rare verb) and interpret 'gives painful birth to,' with a reference to *The Tempest*, II.1.224–6, where the Folio reads *throwes* for *throes*:

> The setting of thine eye and cheek proclaim
> A matter from thee, and a birth indeed
> Which throes thee much to yield.

But here the word means '*causes* thee pain, the pain of a difficult birth,' a sense inadmissible in the context of our passage.

148

Act III, Scene 8

21 like the token'd pestilence Like the plague when its (usually red) spots have appeared on a patient's skin.

29 being loof'd 'Having brought her boat's head toward the wind so that she could sail away'; the word is now spelled 'luff.'

39 he has The F reading *his ha's* is retained by some editors. For support of F reading see J. C. Maxwell, 'Shakespeare's Manuscript of *Antony and Cleopatra*,' *Notes and Queries, 196*, 337.

Act III, Scene 9

23-4 I have lost . . . you Since I have lost the power and authority to order you, I entreat you (to leave me).

36 His sword . . . dancer Since dancers in Shakespeare's day wore a light sword or rapier as ornaments, Antony means that Caesar wore *his* sword for ornament only.

37 lean . . . Cassius Cf. 'Yond Cassius has a lean and hungry look.' *Julius Caesar*, I.2.194.

52-4 How . . . dishonor How I try to remove my shame from your eyes by turning from them and looking at my past which now lies in ruins.

72 schoolmaster Euphronius, the tutor of Antony's children by Cleopatra.

Act III, Scene 10

1SD Thidias So in Folio. Many editors print North's *Thyreus* (Plutarch has *Thyrsus*) throughout the scene.

6SD Enter Ambassador Many editors print 'Enter Euphronius, Ambassador from Antony' and prefix his speeches accordingly.

8-10 as petty . . . sea 'As petty (of as little importance) to his plans and purposes as is the morning dewdrop to those of the ocean.' Some editors read 'its grand sea,' while others take *his* to mean 'its' and interpret: 'to its (the drewdrop's) grand sea, from which it is exhaled.' Another interpretation is: 'to his (Antony's) full tide of prosperity.'

35-6 what thou . . . moves What you think is the meaning and purpose of his every act. What we may forecast concerning his state of mind by observing his present behavior.

Act III, Scene 11

8 nick'd Cut short, like a fool's hair, thereby placing a mark of folly upon it. Cf. 'His man with scissors nicks him like a fool,' *Comedy of Errors*, V.1.175. 'To nick' means also 'to get the better of,' 'to cheat,' a *nick* being 'a winning throw in the game of hazard.' Cf. Arden Shakespeare, p. 139.

113 seel A term taken from falconry and meaning to sew up a hawk's eyes by way of preparing it for the use of the hood.

127–9 O, that . . . herd Cf. Psalm 12:12–13. Antony calls himself a horned cuckold surrounded by Cleopatra's lovers.

147 orbs The nine concentric spheres in which the seven planets, the fixed stars, and the *primum mobile* moved about the earth in the Ptolemaic system. Cf. Cleopatra's line, IV.11.9–10: 'O sun! Burn the great sphere thou mov'st in.'

150 Hipparchus Not a loyal follower. 'This Theophilus was the father of Hipparchus, who was had in great estimation about Antonius. He was the first of all his infranchised bondmen that reuolted from him, and yelded vnto Caesar, and afterwardes went and dwelt at Corinthe.' North, p. 1002.

154 our terrene . . . eclips'd 'Our earthly goddess of the moon, that is, Cleopatra, has changed, darkened, portending evil.' In her final moments Cleopatra takes leave of her planet, the moon, V.2.243–4. Mr. Leslie Hotson interprets 'terrene moon' as the Mediterranean fleet of Antony and Cleopatra which has just been defeated by Caesar's smaller but battle-tested navy. See his *Shakespeare's Sonnets Dated* (London, 1949), pp. 7–8.

197 estridge A goshawk, not ostrich. A dove pecking an ostrich is an incongruous image, whereas a dove pecking a goshawk or falcon is more appropriate, and in fact the expression appears in Shakespeare, 3 *Henry VI*, I.4.40–1:

So cowards fight when they can fly no further;
So doves do peck the falcon's piercing talons.

150

Act IV, Scene 2

8 'Take all' Deliberately ambiguous: 'fight desperately' and 'surrender.'

Act IV, Scene 3

1–24 Brother . . . 'Tis strange 'Furthermore, the selfe same night within a little of midnight, when all the citie was quiet, full of feare, and sorrowe, thinking what would be the issue and ende of this warre: it is said that sodainly they heard a maruelous sweete harmonie of sundrie sortes of instrumentes of musicke, with the crie of a multitude of people, as they had bene dauncing, and had song as they vse in Bacchus feastes, with mouinges and turninges after the maner of Satyres: & it seemed that this daunce went through the city vnto the gate that opened to the enemies, & that all the troupe that made this noise they heard, went out of the city at that gate. Now, such as in reason sought the depth of the interpretation of this wonder, thought that it was the god vnto whom Antonius bare singular deuotion to counterfeate and resemble him, that did forsake them.' North, pp. 1005–6.

16 'Tis . . . Hercules. Although in Plutarch the god here forsaking Antony is Bacchus, Shakespeare substituted Hercules, the more appropriately to forecast Antony's defeat on the morrow. Cf. I.3.84, and North, p. 971: 'Now it had bene a speeche of old time, that the familie of the Antonii were discended from one Anton, the sonne of Hercules, whereof the familie took name.'

Act IV, Scene 4

5–8 Nay . . . must be The Folio prints the whole as a single speech by Cleopatra. See Appendix A, 2.

Act IV, Scene 5

1, 3, 6 Soldier The Folio prefixes these speeches *Eros*, but Shakespeare intended the speaker to be the soldier, who also

has the speeches at ll. 10, 13. That these are all his speeches is
made clear by III.7.61 ff.

19SD **Flourish** Some editors begin Scene 6 here, interrupting
the continuity of action in the field.

30–4 **Alexas . . . him** 'For Alexas Laodician, who was brought
into Antonius house and fauor by meanes of Timagenes, and
afterwards was in greater credit with him, then any other Gre-
cian: (for that he had alway bene one of Cleopatraes ministers
to win Antonius, and to ouerthrow all his good determinations
to vse his wife Octauia well) him Antonius had sent vnto Herodes
King of Ivrie, hoping still to keepe him his frend, that he should
not reuolt from him. But he remained there, and betrayed
Antonius. For where he should haue kept Herodes from reuolting
from him, he perswaded him to turne to Caesar: & trusting
King Herodes, he presumed to come in Caesars presence. Howbeit
Herodes did him no pleasure: for he was presently taken prisoner,
and sent in chaines to his owne contrie, & there by Caesars com-
maundement put to death.' North, p. 1004.

59SD **Alarum** With this stage direction some editors begin
Scene 7.

65–6 **a T . . . an H** Pun on 'ache,' pronounced 'aitch' in
Shakespeare's time when a noun.

Act IV, Scene 6

1SD **Alarum** With this stage direction some editors begin
Scene 8.

Act IV, Scene 7

1 SD **Enter a Sentry** With this stage direction some editors
begin Scene 9.

18 **dried with grief** It was believed that with each sigh the
heart lost a drop of blood. Cf. *Hamlet*, IV.7.123–4: 'And then
this "should" is like a spendthrift sigh That hurts by easing.'

Act IV, Scene 8

1 SD **Enter Antony** With this stage direction some editors
begin Scene 10.

9SD **Enter Caesar** With this stage direction some editors begin Scene 11.

13SD **Enter Antony** With this stage direction some editors begin Scene 12.

17–20 Swallows . . . knowledge 'The admirall galley of Cleopatra, was called Antoniade, in the which there chaunced a maruelous ill signe. Swallowes had bred vnder the poope of her shippe, & there came others after them that draue away the first, & plucked downe their neasts.' Shakespeare simplified the augury, perhaps influenced by North's marginal note: 'An ill signe, foreshewed by swallowes breding in Cleopatraes shippe.' North, p. 999.

41 **my crownet, my chief end** 'My coronet, the chief reward of all my efforts.' 'Crown' was used in the sense of fulfillment, the last, final achievement.

51 **dolts** Some editors read *doits*, in which case they doubtfully interpret *diminitives* as 'small coins.' *Doit* was a copper coin of small value, originally of Dutch origin. See Sir William A. Craigie, *A Dictionary of the Older Scottish Tongue* (London, 1937), *2*, 182. Shakespeare uses the word in *The Tempest*, II.2.33–4: 'When they will not give a doit to relieve a lame beggar.'

57 **shirt of Nessus** A poisoned shirt innocently brought to Hercules by his servant Lichas, which caused him such pain that he threw Lichas to the sky (whence he fell into the sea) and had himself burnt on a pyre on Mount Oeta. Before sending the shirt to her husband, Deianira dipped it in the blood of the Centaur Nessus, recently slain by Hercules, believing the dying Centaur's assurance that she would thereby preserve her husband's love.

Act IV, Scene 9

2 **Telamon** Ajax, son of Telamon, went mad when Achilles' shield was denied him and given instead to Ulysses.

2 **boar of Thessaly** The ferocious boar sent by Artemis to ravage Caledon and slain by Meleager.

4 **To th' monument** 'Furthermore, Cleopatra had long before made many sumptuous tombes and monumentes, as well as for excellencie of workemanshippe, as for height and greatness of

153

building, ioyning hard to the temple of Isis. Thither she caused
to be brought all the treasure & pretious things she had of the
auncient kings her predecessors: as gold, siluer, emerods, pearles,
ebbanie, iuorie, and sinnamon, and besides all that, a maruelous
number of torches, faggots, and flaxe.' North, p. 1005.

Act IV, Scene 10

8 **black . . . pageants** Shows that precede or announce the
coming of night. Extremely elaborate and costly, pageants
honored important events or persons, the best known being the
annual pageant honoring the inauguration of the Lord Mayor of
London.

19–20 **Packed . . . triumph** 'Stacked the cards against me
and in Caesar's favor, and played falsely causing my enemy to
win (*triumph*) and me to lose the glory I had staked.' *Triumph*,
early form of 'trump,' enriches the metaphor by suggesting that
Cleopatra betrayed Antony by playing the wrong card (*false-
play'd*) to Caesar's trump.

108SD **Enter [Dercetas and]** Dercetas probably enters with
the guard. The Folio prefixes speech ll. 116–18 *Dercetus*, that at
l. 119 *Decre.*, and prints *Decretas* at V.1.4SD, and *Dec.* at V.1.6.

Act IV, Scene 11

38SD **They heave . . . Cleopatra** The physical problems involved in raising the dying Antony to the upper stage represent-
ing Cleopatra's monument may be in fact solved by a description
of the same action in Samuel Daniel's 1607 version of *Cleopatra*.
Miss Joan Rees offers the attractive theory that Daniel's description is a reminiscence of an actual production of *Antony
and Cleopatra*. For Daniel's passage and further comments see
Joan Rees, 'An Elizabethan Eyewitness of *Antony and Cleopatra*,' *Shakespeare Survey, 6* (1953), 91–3. Cf. also Roy Walker,
'*Antony and Cleopatra*,' (London) *Times Literary Supplement*,
May 29, 1953, p. 349.

39 **when** So in F. Pope and later editors print *where*. The
sense of the F reading is: 'Die after you have lived once more,'
an interpretation supported by 'quicken with kissing.'

52–9 The miserable . . . vanquish'd 'When he had dronke, he earnestly prayed her, and perswaded her, that she would seeke to saue her life, if she could possible, without reproache and dishonor: and that chiefly she should trust Proculeius aboue any man else about Caesar. And as for him selfe, that she should not lament nor sorowe for the miserable chaunge of his fortune at the end of his dayes: but rather that she would thinke him the more fortunate, for the former triumphes & honors he had receiued, considering that while he liued he was the noblest and greatest Prince of the world, & that now he was ouercome, not cowardly, but valiantly, a Romane by an other Romane.' North, pp. 1006–7.

66 pole Another interpretation, given by Schmidt and some editors, is 'lodestar,' a sense made acceptable by IV.10.111, above.

74 in Contracted, weakly stressed form of *even*, which appears also as *e'ne, e'ene,* or *ev'n.* See Kökeritz, *Shakespeare's Pronunciation,* pp. 203–4.

Act V, Scene 1

29, 33 Agrippa The Folio assigns these two speeches to Dolabella, who in fact is not on the stage, having left it at l. 4. Theobald and subsequent editors assign them to Agrippa.

78 writings 'Then he called for all his frendes, and shewed them the letters Antonius had written to him, and his aunsweres also sent him againe, during their quarrell and strife: & how fiercely and prowdly the other answered him, to all iust and reasonable matters he wrote vnto him.' North, p. 1007.

Act V, Scene 2

23 Make your . . . freely Entrust yourself and your fortunes wholly and without fear.

27 will pray . . . kindness Will ask for help in looking for opportunities to do kind acts.

34SD Roman . . . Cleopatra This incident, as well as the entire scene, takes place inside the monument, and it is now generally agreed that it was acted on the main stage. See The

Arden Shakespeare, pp. 251–7; C. W. Hodges, *The Globe Restored*
(London, Ernest Benn, 1953), pp. 59–60.

35–6 **You see . . . come** Although the Folio heads these lines
Pro., some editors have assigned them to Gallus, who presum-
ably leads the soldiers who surprise Cleopatra. Such a drastic
emendation was called for by the necessity to eliminate the
duplication of the speech heading *Pro.*, and the choice of Gallus
was dictated by the fact that in the preceding scene Caesar sends
him to the monument shortly after Proculeius. The editors have
been influenced also by North's account of the incident, although
there Proculeius is the one who surprises Cleopatra while Gallus
holds her in conversation. It is possible that Gallus does lead
the soldiers who surprise Cleopatra, although there is no evidence
in the Folio for his presence on the scene until l. 110. But if he
does appear on the stage he must remain mute, and the lines in
question must be spoken by Proculeius, for the duplication of
the speech heading was caused not by careless speech distribution
but by the omission of at least a speech. And for such an assumption we have good evidence. The duplication occurs at the precise
point in the text where a crucial stage direction should be forth-
coming, and it is reasonable to assume that such a stage direction
appeared in the poet's manuscript. For in the matter of stage
directions, both as to frequency and detail, our play is almost
unique. And the absence of a stage direction here suggests
strongly that something else in the manuscript may have been
omitted as well at this point, perhaps a speech or two. Mr.
Ridley's view (Arden ed., p. 254) that Proculeius is unaware of
Caesar's little plot against Cleopatra and that therefore the lines
are spoken by Gallus, who is privy to it, must be rejected. Proculeius could not mistake Caesar's lines addressed to him before
he leaves for Cleopatra's monument (V.1.64–8):

> give her what comforts
> The quality of her passion shall require,
> Lest in her greatness by some mortal stroke
> She do defeat us. For her life in Rome
> Would be eternal in our triumph.

On the other hand, sending Gallus seems like an afterthought, and Caesar gives him no instructions whatever.

88–90 his delights . . . liv'd in He kept himself above (superior to) the pleasures in which he lived just as the dolphin keeps its back above the water.

98–100 yet . . . quite Yet to imagine an actual Antony, to accept him as a product of Nature, would be to place Nature above fancy since he would excel (and put to shame) even fancy's most outlandish creations.

223 Some . . . greatness 'Some boy actor with squeaking voice will burlesque my greatness.' Until the second half of the 17th century female parts were acted by boys on the English stage.

291–2 The luck . . . wrath Caesar's good fortune, the sort of excessively good luck which the envious gods use as an excuse (since good fortune may lead to pride) for striking a man (with such luck) down.

294–6 my other . . . life Since of the four elements (earth, fire, air, water) thought to constitute the human body only air and fire were associated with immortality, Cleopatra bequeaths the other two to mortal, that is human, life.

359–61 for her physician . . . die 'So when she had dayly made diuers and sundrie proofes, she found none of all them she had proued so fit, as the biting of an Aspicke, the which only causeth a heauines of the head, without swounding or complaining, and bringeth a great desire also to sleepe, with a little swet in the face, and so by litle and litle taketh away the sences and vitall powers, no liuing creature perceiuing that the pacientes feele any paine.' North, p. 1004.

APPENDIX A

1. The Date

The earliest record of *Antony and Cleopatra* appears in the Stationers' Register, where under date of May 20, 1608, Edward Blount, the publisher, entered his copy of the play. On the basis of indirect evidence, however, it appears that the play had been completed a year or two earlier. For instance, it probably served as the model for the revision which Samuel Daniel made in his play *Cleopatra* before republishing it in 1607. In this revised edition of his play Daniel replaced much of the relation of events by dialogue, gave greater parts to Iras and Charmian, and introduced Diomedes and Dercetas, the latter in the scene in which he brings Antony's sword to Caesar. Daniel had published *Cleopatra* in 1594, 1599, 1601, and 1602, but only in the edition of 1607 did he make the alterations which brought a portion of his play nearer Shakespeare's tragedy. There is good reason to believe, then, that *Antony and Cleopatra* was the impetus and model for Daniel's revisions, and that therefore it must have been completed in or before 1607 (see IV.11.38 N).

Echoes of *Antony and Cleopatra* can be heard also in Barnabe Barnes' *The Devil's Charter*, first acted on February 2, 1607, and printed in October of the same year. In a brief passage of the play reference is made to 'Aspiks,' 'Cleopatra's birds,' 'Egyptian slime,' 'Nylus,' 'Ptolemies wife'; and there is the stage direction, 'He putteth to either of their brests an Aspike.' Such echoes may not constitute proof but they support the view that *Antony and Cleopatra* had appeared in 1607 if not earlier. How much earlier the play had been written can be fixed by the dates of two plays, from one of which Shakespeare seems to have borrowed Antony's image of the dragonish cloud (IV.10.2–8). The two plays are George Chapman's *Monsieur D'Olive* (1606) and his *Bussy D'Ambois* (1607). In the latter play appears the passage:

> and like empty clouds,
> In which our faulty apprehensions forge
> The forms of dragons, lions, elephants,
> When they hold no proportion.[1]

1. *The Plays of George Chapman*, ed. T. M. Parrott (London, George Routledge & Sons, 1910), III.1.23–6.

Perhaps more appropriate as Shakespeare's source is a passage in the earlier play where, as in Antony's image, the central thought is the decline of great men's fortunes:

> Our great men
> Like to a mass of clouds that now seem like
> An elephant, and straightways like an ox,
> And then a mouse. . . .[2]

Since the dates of the two plays are 1606 and 1607, we may fix 1606 as the earliest date for *Antony and Cleopatra*. And there is support for such conclusion from internal evidence. On the basis of metrical tests *Antony and Cleopatra* follows *Macbeth*, whose date is 1606. The date of the play, then, is 1606 or 1607.

2. The Text

Though Edward Blount entered his copy in the Stationers' Register in 1608, the play does not appear to have been printed until much later, and the earliest text we possess is that of the First Folio (1623). The probability is strong that this text was set up from a fair copy of Shakespeare's manuscript before its excessive length had been trimmed for stage performance. In support of this theory may be cited the peculiarly Shakespearean misspellings, misprints, and colloquial abbreviations in the text which are duplicated in good quartos or even in Folio texts believed to be based on Shakespeare's manuscripts (New Cambridge Shakespeare, ed. J. D. Wilson, pp. 124–30). Furthermore the stage directions are so precise and demanding, even fussy, and at the same time impracticable, that they appear to be the work of the author rather than those of a promptbook used in an actual performance.

The view that the text was not based on that of a promptbook is supported by the presence of textual irregularities which the prompter might be thought to have eliminated. For instance he would have assigned the speeches at IV.5.1,3,6 to *Soldier*, not to *Eros*, and he would not have retained Dolabella as the speaker at V.1.29,33, since he is not on the stage at the time. It is also likely that he would have eliminated the duplication of the speech

2. *Ibid.*, II.2.91–4.

prefix *Eno.* at II.7.135,139, and of *Proc.* at V.2.32,35. These are errors due to forgetfulness on the part of Shakespeare or his scribe, and though they appear insignificant, the prompter could not have allowed them to stand since they would have obscured the meaning of the passages involved.

The text contains other irregularities, most of which may be laid to the compositor. In I.2.67–73 he took six lines from Charmian's speech and set them up as a separate speech and prefixed it *Alexas*. The name *Alexas* occurs in Charmian's speech, but the compositor mistook it for a speech prefix, printed it as such, and transferred to it that portion of Charmian's speech which followed it. On the other hand the speech prefix at IV.4.5–8 shows the compositor making the reverse error. Here he mistook the speech prefix *Anthony* for part of Cleopatra's speech and printed:

> *Cleo.* Nay, Ile helpe too, *Anthony*,
> What's this for? Ah let be, let be, thou art
> The Armourer of my heart: False, false this, this,
> Sooth-law Ile helpe: Thus it must bee.

Anthony was the prefix for the speech 'Ah . . . this, this,' which Shakespeare probably wrote in the margin of his manuscript. The compositor literally inserted it between two of Cleopatra's speeches; and having eliminated one speech prefix, he was forced to cancel a second to avoid duplication. Consequently, he struck off the prefix *Cleo.* from the line 'Sooth-law . . . bee,' and added the line to the rest, making one speech out of three.

One last error in speech prefixes may claim comment. In II.1, where Menas and Menecrates appear together, the Folio prefixes *Mene.* all speeches not spoken by Pompey or Varrius, the other two characters in the scene. This, however, renders Menas mute, although two of Pompey's speeches (ll. 32–9, 43–53) are addressed to him and he is three times called by name in them. Far from being mute, then, Menas may claim those speeches prefixed *Mene.* which Pompey seems to be answering, that is, ll. 17–18, 19, 39–43. The speeches have been reassigned by editors in a variety of ways, the least satisfactory being that in the New Cambridge Shakespeare, where Professor Dover Wilson, following Johnson's hint, assigned all speeches prefixed *Mene.* to Menas. Professor Wilson believes that *Mene.* stands for Menas since the latter is once called Menes in the Folio (II.7.17SD). But even if his name were Menes, the argument would not be conclusive since *Mene.* could stand for either name. Nor is it likely that Shakespeare would have prefixed Menas' (or Menes') speeches *Mene.* in a scene shared with Menecrates. Even in II.6 and 7, where Menecrates does not appear, Menas' speeches are prefixed *Men.*

It may be argued that the compositor failed to distinguish between *Mene.* and *Men.* in Shakespeare's manuscript, and having set up *Mene.* for the first two speeches, he proceeded to do the same for the rest. That the speeches belong to two different, if not opposite, personalities is suggested by their content and tone. In the first two Menecrates calmly and philosophically recommends prudence and patience to the overconfident Pompey, whereas in the remaining speeches the pragmatic Menas thrusts before his master urgent facts of military and political nature. Menas is the pirate who in a later scene offers to slit the triumvirs' throats so that his master might rule the world alone. To such a character one is scarcely tempted to attribute the lines:

> we, ignorant of ourselves
> Beg often our own harms, which the wise powers
> Deny us for our good; so find we profit
> By losing of our prayers.

The text of the present edition is based on the First Folio, to which it adheres in all important matters. Of minor changes, the most important deal with punctuation and spelling, both of which have been modernized in accordance with the general editorial policy laid down in the Preface. In the matter of proper names a distinction has been made between spelling and form: the latter is retained throughout, whereas the spelling has been slightly changed in a few cases. Among proper names whose form is preserved is *Mesena* (II.2.165), which editors unnecessarily change to *Misenum*, although it is clear that Shakespeare is following North's spelling of *Misena*. Also restored is the Shakespearean *Thidias* (III.10) which in many editions is

metamorphosed into *Thyreus* (Plutarch, *Thyrsus*). Shakespeare
is not as careless in his spelling of proper names as we are oc-
casionally asked to believe. In our play he reproduces so accu-
rately such difficult names as Hipparchus, Proculeius, Seleucus,
Ventidius (Ventigius), and Menecrates (also Menacrates) that
when his spelling differs from North's we may reasonably con-
clude that the compositor is reponsible for most, if not all, such
variations. For instance there is no reason why Shakespeare
should have written *Orades* instead of *Orodes*, *Medena* instead of
Modena; the only plausible explanation for such spelling is that
the compositor misread Shakespeare's manuscript. Consequently
I have emended the Folio spelling of such names, as for instance
Towrus to *Taurus*, *Brandusium* to *Brundusium*, *Orades* to *Orodes*,
Medena to *Modena*, *Licoania* to *Lycaonia*, *Action* (*Actiom*) to
Actium, *Cidrus* (*Sidnis*) to *Cydnus*. I have also changed *Anthony*
to *Antony*, since the latter represents more clearly the pronunci-
ation and is in fact the spelling given in *Julius Caesar*.

Another matter in which the present text adheres to the Folio
is lineation. Much has been said in defense of regularizing what
appears to be mislineation in the text of Shakespearean plays.
In such defense the arguments are based on the unwarranted
assumption that in all verse passages, even in the late plays,
Shakespeare wrote nothing but precise iambic pentameter. That
this is not so the text of *Antony and Cleopatra* makes very clear.
In a play whose pervasive quality is spaciousness and freedom
we are not surprised to find what may be called irregular lines;
for it is clear that here, as elsewhere, the dramatist was concerned
far more with rhythm and pause than with metrical consistency.
Yet editors have rearranged his lines even when the change involved was a minute one. For instance, in the opening scene of
the play the Folio prints ll. 52–4 in the following manner:

> No messenger but thine, and all alone tonight
> We'll wander through the streets, and note
> The qualities of people.

It is true that l. 52 stretches beyond the regular five feet. But it
is no great matter; and certainly if we read *messenger* as dissyllabic

the line may pass for a respectable pentameter. Some editors, however, print the lines to read as follows:

> No messenger but thine, and all alone
> Tonight we'll wander through the streets, and note
> The qualities of people.

Since both lines (52–3) can be read as pentameters (we may read *We'll* 'We will') the change is unnecessary; but it is also unfortunate, and indeed unacceptable, since by placing *tonight* at the beginning of l. 53 editors give it the primary emphasis and furthermore make it modify *we'll wander* exclusively, whereas in fact it modifies *all alone* as well and rhythmically belongs with it. Finally, what reason can the compositor have had for making such a small change in Shakespeare's manuscript? If the Folio reading is what Shakespeare wrote, it should remain inviolate.

A similar instance is I.3.101–2, which the Folio prints as follows:

> Be strew'd before your feet:
> *Ant.* Let vs go.
> Come: Our separation so abides and flies

Finding l. 102 excessively long, Pope and subsequent editors regularized it by adding its first foot to the end of l. 101. Again, it is difficult to discover for what reason the compositor would have made such a small change, assuming that Shakespeare wrote *Come* at the end of l. 101. If, as we learn elsewhere, the compositor was troubled by long pentameters, some of them too long for his column, why should he have lengthened l. 102 by adding a word taken from a half-line? On the contrary, he often divides a long pentameter into half-lines, as for instance I.3.33, which the Folio prints as two lines:

> But bid farewell, and goe:
> When you sued staying,

This is the compositor's most frequent departure from Shakespeare's lineation, and in the present text such half-lines are reunited into a single pentameter.

Not all short lines, however, can be so explained and regularized. To be sure, it is generally safe to combine into a single pentameter two consecutive half-lines. But what of single short lines? Take for instance two such lines separated by a regular pentameter, as in II.2.16–19:

> *Ant.* If we compose well heere, to Parthia:
> Harke *Ventidius.*
> *Caesar.* I do not know Mecenas, aske *Agrippa.*
> *Lep.* Noble Friends:

Since the passage apparently violates 18th-century prosody, editors have regularized it into the following:

> *Ant.* If we compose well here, to Parthia:
> Hark, Ventidius.
> *Caesar.*   I do not know,
> Maecenas; ask Agrippa.
> *Lep.*   Noble friends,

The change is, of course, unnecessary and indeed unfortunate, for the Folio reading is unquestionably superior, and for the following reasons. First, 'Hark, Ventidius' is a short line not a half-line; that is, it is not the first half of a pentameter. It is independent of the following speech, and in fact its brevity is intended to suggest an awkward pause between the two speeches, perhaps even the distance separating Caesar and Antony on the stage. Second, the regularization breaks up l. 18, which is a precise iambic pentameter: it interrupts the flow of its musical phrasing by separating *Maecenas* from the preceding clause, with which it surely belongs. And finally the regularization disregards the long pause very clearly marked by the colon at the end of the short line 'Noble friends,' a pause which indicates Lepidus' apprehension and hesitation. The phrase commands a pause, it would seem, for its import must go home to both Antony and Caesar. The two words are not, I believe, a portion of the preceding pentameter but a line in themselves.

Another irregularity in the Folio text is the presence of prose passages which, we are convinced, Shakespeare wrote as verse. Why the compositor made the change is not always clear, but in most cases he did so to conserve space. Now and then he refuses to set up half lines but instead runs them together with a portion

of the following pentameter. But in doing so he loses control of
the verse lines and is therefore forced to print the remainder of
the speech as prose. An instance of such practice is the following
passage (I.5.62–7):

> *Alex.* I Madam, twenty seuerall Messengers.
> Why do you send so thicke?
> *Cleo.* Who's borne that day when I forget to send
> to *Anthonie*, shall dye a Begger. Inke and paper *Char-*
> *mian*. Welcome my good *Alexas*. Did I *Charmian*, e-
> uer loue Caesar so?
> *Char.* Oh that braue Caesar!

In fairness to the compositor it must be said that he may have
been confused by revisions in the margin of Shakespeare's manuscript. Whatever the cause of the Folio lineation, I believe that
we may profitably rearrange the lines on the assumption that
Cleopatra's speech was written in verse. Such an assumption is
strongly supported not only by the context but also by Charmian's half-line which is of sufficient length to complete the
terminal half-line of Cleopatra's speech. A similar instance is
II.1.1–6, a portion of which the Folio prints as prose:

> *Pom.* If the great Gods be iust, they shall assist
> The deeds of iustest men.
> *Mene.* Know worthy *Pompey*, that what they do de-
> lay, they not deny.
> *Pom.* Whiles we are sutors to their Throne, decayes
> the thing we sue for.
> *Mene.* We ignorant of our selues,
> Begge often our owne harmes, which the wise Powres

Here we may assume that the lines printed as prose were written
in verse by Shakespeare, and for the following reasons. The
ellipsis in the second speech and the inversion in the third are
strong evidence against prose; and the initial half-line 'We ignorant of our selues' presupposes a terminal half-line in the
preceding speech, since no other reason can be cited for its
length. Going back over the passage we may assume that 'Know
worthy *Pompey*' is a half-line completing the terminal half-line
of the preceding speech. But the compositor again refuses to

give it a whole line in his column and instead adds to it a portion of the following pentameter. Unfortunately in doing so he is forced to print the remainder of the speech in prose; and having disturbed the verse lines of one speech, he proceeds to do the same in the following speech as well. Then he comes upon a familiar landmark, the initial half-line of Menecrates' speech in l. 5, which he prints correctly as well as the remainder of the passage.

It is clear, then, that convincing reasons may be adduced for preserving the Folio lineation of most apparently mislineated passages and in effect for seeing that it is superior to any other; and also for regularizing the lineation of a few speeches where we may be certain the compositor departed from Shakespeare's manuscript. We may not, in other words, follow a blanket policy but must treat each passage separately.

Finally it will be seen that the present edition dispenses with the traditional act and scene divions which in other editions mark the action of the play. Aside from being absent in the Folio text and therefore without authority, such formal divisions are scarcely admissible in a play where fluidity of scene and smoothness of action are of first importance. However, in order to facilitate reference to lines in this and other editions and to critical works, I have noted the act and scene divisions at the top of each page and again in the glosses. Since I have combined the battle scenes in Acts III and IV and since in general I have retained the Folio lineation, my line numbering is slightly different from that of other editions.

In preparing the present edition I have received aid from other editors of *Antony and Cleopatra*, particularly from J. D. Wilson, M. R. Ridley, G. L. Kittredge (Boston, Ginn and Co., 1941), and H. H. Furness (Philadelphia, J. B. Lippincott Co., 1907). To all I wish to acknowledge my debt. And I am especially grateful to the general editors of the Yale Shakespeare, Professors Charles T. Prouty and Helge Kökeritz, for their help and kindness to me.

APPENDIX B

Sources

The source of *Antony and Cleopatra* is Plutarch's *Lives of the Noble Grecians and Romans Compared Together*, first printed in 1579. Although North did not go to the Greek original but instead turned into English Jacques Amyot's French translation, his version of the *Lives* shows a startling fidelity to the original. And it appears that this fidelity may have been due in part to the instantaneous attraction North must have felt for Plutarch, whom he reverently calls 'Philosopher and Historiographer.' The attraction, with its attendant fidelity, was repeated a few years later when Shakespeare laid his hand on North's translation. As an additional source a small claim has been advanced for Samuel Daniel's play *Cleopatra* (1595), and it is possible that Shakespeare borrowed a few details from it. But from Plutarch he took all the incidents which make up the drama of Antony's decline and death, and he took also the main characters and much of the language, this last coming to him in the gorgeous prose of North's Elizabethan translation.

In reorganizing the events into a tragedy Shakespeare made no use of those incidents which dealt with the rise in Antony's fortunes, although he often makes reference to them in order to establish the hero's nobility and achievements. He selected, abridged, and rearranged only those episodes which in some way affected or reflected Antony's relationship with Cleopatra, for, unlike Plutarch, he was composing a tragedy in which two lovers played equal parts. It follows, then, that Shakespeare established his own balance in the roles of these two and consequently redistributed the concentration of interest.

Plutarch's main characters served Shakespeare as prototypes which he elaborated by means of emphasis and detail, but the elaboration did not always involve profound change. For instance, in depicting Antony Shakespeare did not find it necessary to alter the lines of the character he had found in North. Plutarch, no less than Shakespeare, was primarily concerned with the enigma of character, in the case of Antony with the juxtaposition in him of strength and weakness in their highest degree. To

167

Plutarch it seemed that Antony illustrated a saying by Plato that 'from great minds, both great vertues and great vices do procede'; and he presented him, as Shakespeare did in the play, in what might be called a tragic equilibrium, a balance between his virtues and the ignoble deeds by which he destroyed himself. But there is this difference between the two characterizations: whereas Plutarch's Antony in the end bows before the moral principles he has violated, Shakespeare's reaffirms his adherence to the values he has espoused, the values by which he has lived, loved, and apparently lost.

In the characterization of Cleopatra Shakespeare departed significantly from Plutarch, who saw her only as another agent in Antony's tragedy. In Plutarch she is not a tragic character: the tragedy is Antony's and his alone. Shakespeare, on the other hand, elevates her to that position, and in Act V presents her in the process of apprehending the tragic experience. But the tragic dignity with which she is invested does not change her. On the contrary, the supreme fascination of the closing moments derives from the juxtaposition in her of the alluring temptress and the tragic heroine. Their tragic vision, then, changes neither Antony nor Cleopatra, and in this particular fact lies Shakespeare's most significant departure from Plutarch. Whereas the philosophic historiographer presents the world of Egypt in opposition to the world of Rome and in the death of Antony and Cleopatra emphasizes the operation of the moral laws they have violated, the dramatist merely juxtaposes the two worlds, and against the death of his hero and heroine he places the triumph of their devotion to the principles by which they have lived.

The most striking correspondence between the play and its source is in language. North's prose, not far removed from poetry, came conveniently to Shakespeare's hand, and he was content on occasion to lift whole passages of it and transfer them to his play. For instance, Enobarbus' description of Cleopatra's first visit to Antony seems little more than a transcription in blank verse of North's lines:

> Therefore when she was sent vnto by diuers letters, both
> from Antonius him selfe, and also from his frendes, she
> made so light of it, and mocked Antonius so much, that

she disdained to set forward otherwise, but to take her barge in the riuer of Cydnus, the poope whereof was of gold, the sailes of purple, and the owers of siluer, which kept stroke in rowing after the sounde of the musicke of flutes, howboyes, citherns, violls, and such other instruments as they played vpon in the barge. And now for the person of her selfe: she was layed vnder a pauillion of cloth of gold of tissue, apparelled and attired like the goddesse Venus, commonly drawen in picture: and hard by her, on either hand of her, pretie faire boyes apparelled as painters doe set forth god Cupide, with litle fannes in their hands, with the which they fanned wind vpon her. Her Ladies and gentlewomen also, the fairest of them were apparelled like the nymphes Nereides (which are the mermaides of the waters) and like the Graces, some stearing the helme, others tending the tackle and ropes of the barge, out of the which there came a wonderfull passing sweete sauor of perfumes, that perfumed the wharfes side, pestered with innumerable multitudes of people. Some of them followed the barge all alongest the riuers side: others also ranne out of the citie to see her comming in. So that in thend, there ranne such multitudes of people one after an other to see her, that Antonius was left post alone in the market place, in his Imperiall seate to geue audience: and there went a rumor in the peoples mouthes, that the goddesse Venus was come to play with the god Bacchus, for the generall good of all Asia. (Pp. 981–2.)

A comparison of the passage with II.2.196–224 of the play will show how much and how minutely Shakespeare borrowed from this description. But it will show also that Shakespeare's additions, though few, make a great deal of difference. In describing Cleopatra's barge Shakespeare makes the winds *lovesick* with the perfumed sails, and the water *amorous* of the oars' strokes. Another fanciful touch by which Shakespeare vivifies the scene occurs in the description of the deserted Antony. Plutarch says that so many people had gone out to see Cleopatra 'that Antonius was left post alone in the market place to geue audience.' This in Shakespeare becomes:

                                          and Antony,
            Enthron'd i' th' market-place, did sit alone,
            Whistling to th' air.

Other instances of verbal correspondence may be cited, among
them the Soothsayer's colloquy with Antony (II.3.10–32), Antony's dying speech (IV.11.52–60), and the Seleucus episode
(V.2.141–76). Such borrowing from his prose may be a compliment to North, but it is not, of course, a defect in the play. The
passages borrowed were elevated to blank verse, and they were
so vitally and smoothly fitted to their contexts that they give
the reader no reason to question their origin.

APPENDIX C

Reading List

M. R. RIDLEY, ed., *Antony and Cleopatra*, Arden Shakespeare, London, Methuen and Co., 1954.

J. D. WILSON, ed., *Antony and Cleopatra*, New Cambridge, Cambridge, Cambridge University Press, 1950.

A. C. BRADLEY, 'Antony and Cleopatra,' in *Oxford Lectures on Poetry*, London, Macmillan and Co., 1909.

LORD DAVID CECIL, *Antony and Cleopatra*, Glasgow University Publications, vol. *58* (1943).

H. GRANVILLE-BARKER, *Prefaces to Shakespeare*, 2d series, London, Sidgwick and Jackson, Ltd., 1927.

W. FARNHAM, *Shakespeare's Tragic Frontier*, Berkeley, University of California Press, 1950, pp. 139–205.

G. W. KNIGHT, *The Imperial Theme*, London, H. Milford, 1931.

M. W. MACCALLUM, *Shakespeare's Roman Plays and Their Background*, London, Macmillan and Co., 1925.

NORTH'S *Plutarch*, London, 1579.